# Trip

# Back

Also by Nirvan Hope

*Three Seasons of Bees*
*and*
*Other Natural and Unnatural Things:*
*A Pacific Northwest Journal*

*Gypsy Soup: a novel*

*Love and the Infinite*
*Poems 1992-1998*

# Trip Back

*Windows to the Past*

NIRVAN HOPE

ISBN: 9781091924109

First Edition Published 2019

Front Cover Photo: 3 Church Street © 2012 Nirvan Hope
Cover Design: Nirvan Hope
Author Photo: Madir Thackeray

For my mother

who
inspired my first desire to write

when our mirrors become windows,
the light won't just bounce around
a room of imagined dreams,
they will yield to the harmony
we sang before time began,
that still sings softly in our depths.

when our mirrors become windows,
we will open them to the world
and breathe in the sweetness
of our natural born freedom,
remembering the moments
that birthed this ancient labyrinth.

when mirrors become windows,
we will be able to finally share
the art of our deepest dreams,
the music of our purest heart,
the words of our clearest mind,
and the echoes will ring no more.

—YOSSARIAN KELLEY

# Contents

Introduction

Acknowledgements

About the Author

# Introduction

EVERYONE has a story to tell. And not only one—many, many. Here are some of mine.

This is not a book of essays or poems or teachings, just scraps of personal memory told in a smorgasbord of styles, a patchwork collage of stories, scenes, and recollections from a fully-lived life only touched on with this collection. It is a mish-mash of memoir. I experimented with what I call 'prose versification'. Some pieces might contain insights, some are moods or descriptions of places and people, all distilled from time stretched back and forth from different periods and understandings. There is no way I could contain the unruly octopus of my life within any orderly boundaries; many wandering periods are only hinted at, while other long periods are excluded entirely. Only one name has been changed.

The longest piece in the collection, "Trip Back" is an exploration of relationship to my family of origin through memories fleshed out around the skeleton of a visit to England in 2012, a journey that ended with a surprising revelation. Other fragments reflect people and places or events that touched my world one way or another, and some might hint at why I didn't take my GED until I was almost fifty years old.

My life has been filled with contradiction and contrast. In no particular order: from damp gray England, to heat and color of sub-Saharan Africa; from work on the top floor of the NY Stock Exchange, to single mother on welfare; from travel and living in a covered wagon, to travel on six continents (living on four); from city living, to a raspberry farm; from many love affairs, marriage and relationships, to celibacy; from a home by the sea, to a mountain cabin; from President of a non-profit, to anonymous house cleaner; from communes and communities, to living alone; from forest life, to suburbia; from artist, to cubicle slave; from inheritance to bankruptcy; from being listed as a member of a terrorist organization, to selling honey at farmers markets.

However, the glue that holds my life together is none of those extremes. It is the blessings of a day-to-day life of relative inner stability, good friends, communities, family, the gift of good health, resilience, optimism, meditation, living close to nature, and a good work ethic that give me the freedom to pursue my creativity, and in this case, to share some stories from the ongoing journey of my life.

It is my hope these memoir pieces will entertain, spark the imagination, and conjure a few memories for reclaiming, owning, and perhaps sharing some of your stories with friends, family, or the world.

May it be so.

# 1. The Giving of Bliss

Two days of heat and endless ocean
from our last port-of-call,
Los Palmas, in the Canary Isles,
the rusted banana boat chugs closer to the equator,
steaming down the Atlantic coast of Africa.

Shattering the ocean's rolling surface,
sun reflections flash blinding streaks.
Everywhere, water, sun and sky;
no land in sight.

I lean tanned arms on railings
thick with layers of sea-stained paint;
my tongue licks salt lips,
hair juts stiff from salt water swimming,
sea smells permeate every sense.

From the stern of the P and O liner
en route from Liverpool to Lagos
wake rolls and folds
in ever-widening Vs to the horizon line.

Beside the mammoth hull,
dazzling arcs of flying fish leap,
dripping, glistening, iridescent
with spray and light.
I run from stern to prow,
race the finned flyers,
watch their sleek bodies speed
ahead into the distance.

Sharp curves of the ship's bow
slice through tropical water,
carving a passage ever closer
to a new life in Africa.
And, like the sparkling fish that fly and dive
ahead of the ship, and fly and dive again,
I, too, speed ahead to slice new water.

Below deck, in the small cabin
shared with my mother,
a gray portable typewriter sits
on a fold-down table under a porthole.

Since the vessel left Gibraltar,
after four years of idyllic Mediterranean life,
my mother has kept a journal of our voyage,
planning to turn memories
into a book of travel and future tropical life.
Each evening, under dim table-lamp light,
she stays up late,
typewriter keys clicking in rhythm with
the hypnotic drone of engine throb
and slapping waves.

When I peek from covers of my narrow bunk
and watch her type,
I can tell that she is happy.
The writing puts a dreamy smile on her face.
A warm invisible glow fills the cabin.

When she finishes typing for the night,
she straightens a small stack of word-covered
sheets beside the typewriter.
She leaves a page in the carriage
with four or five typed lines,
a prompt for the next day
when she will describe in detail
the next idea, event, or scene.
She smiles, picks up the printed pile,
pats the pages into neat conformity,
places them back on the table,
leans over and lightly kisses
the top of my head as I feign sleep.

I am six, going on seven.
I want to know what it is like to write
what she has written.
But more than my desire to write,
it is the feeling of bliss that flows from her,
flooding the room while she types,
that I want to know and own.

Why don't I sit at that typewriter
and add to the story of our ocean voyage?
Perhaps then, I will know that bliss.

"Okay," she says when I mention it at breakfast,
"go ahead. It's a lovely idea."
That afternoon, I sneak down to the cabin
rest my fingertips on the cool metal keypads,
and peck out: "We ate breakfast. I ate fried eggs.
I swam in the pool. We had lunch."

Then my mind goes blank.
I think of nothing interesting to say,
incapable of describing scenes of my first lines here.
My stunted six-year-old vocabulary
never comes close.
And I definitely don't experience bliss.
How does my mother cover so many pages
and look so happy?
Instead of a dreamy smile,
my chin trembles as I hold back tears.

My mother encourages me to write.
But day after day the same paper
sits silent in the typewriter carriage.
I don't attempt to write another sentence,
ashamed by my utter lack of skill with words.

The paper lies in wait,
taunting me the rest of the journey.
My mother doesn't write more either.
She never continues the book
and later must have thrown away
the few pages already written.
Only years later did she write again,
letters to newspapers.

As a teenager, perhaps from those
gifts of my mother's bliss,
from guilt at stemming her flow of words,
shame at my verbal inadequacy,
or mostly as an excuse for wild adventures,
I often promised my mother
I would one day be a writer.

As an adult, whenever I returned
to the shelter of her home,
broken or ecstatic, sick or successful,
from the other side of the world,
with a man in tow,
or with a fatherless child,
I told her I was gathering material
for the books that I would one day write.

But no more 'we ate breakfast',
'we had lunch' kind of writing.
I promised myself someday I would make up
for everything my mother had not written,
and return the bliss that she had gifted to me.

# 2. Gibraltar

This tree, this hideaway,
could be your childhood secret place,
where figs hang sweet and ripe from twisted branches,
and leathery leaves stretch sheltering hands
protecting from the summer sun.

Climb inside the branches,
lean back against the heart/trunk,
gaze to where clarkia blazes shades of pink
from palest dawn to sunset crimson,
where geraniums, scarlet red,
decorate each patch and cranny of sun-soaked earth,
where red hot pokers reign along a wall
holding the terrace below your home
on a slope of the Gibraltar Rock.

Happy in your fig tree,
breathe the spice of geranium leaves,
watch honey bees, butterflies,
work their garden diligence.
Reach up, pluck a ripe fig,
avoiding sticky white sap
from where the fruit has grown.
Bite into the juicy tenderness.

The gritty crunch of tiny seeds
mixes with distant laughter,
zizzle and click of crickets,
Spanish voices from downhill,
and further down, a braying donkey.

The light is sharp and clear.
On a breeze, cool and salty against your skin,
Mediterranean smells rise from a steep cliff
that drops to a strip of sparkled ocean
between Europe and the desert hills of Africa.

Many steps and hairpin bends above the town,
days weave long and luxurious,
close to where wild apes
wander and pilfer from unwary travelers.

With endless hours of sunshine,
you breathe the freedom
of long beaches and a warm sea:
Bullers beach, Tarifa, Sandy Bay, Hitarrez.
Rocks to climb, tide pools that reveal
their hidden ocean wealth,
the ebb and flow of ripple and wave.

You run, you splash, you tumble.
Pulled under by a frothing wave,
you're lifted safe by strong and loving arms.
Running on hot sand, digging and building
castles with your little fingers,
burying legs in cool sand,
sand blowing, sand in hair,
sand under finger nails,
a sandy picnic lunch.

With a background soundtrack of fiery flamenco,
weaving Moroccan melodies,

saffron-scented food, bougainvillea,
a Spanish cook and nanny
with smiling affection
a nod of her head,
and a little pinch of cheek
whispers "linda, linda, mucha linda"
(my name was Linda then).

This was my childhood paradise.

# 3. Student Number 43

Daily, bush-telegraph drums weave intricate rhythms,
a hypnotic background to reading, writing, and arithmetic,
but this morning there's no weaving of melodic language,
news of arrivals, departures, planting and harvest.
This morning, drum-talk explodes.
Louder and louder, angry, punched, staccato drum-slaps
echo from the marketplace by Kaduna Sacred Heart school.
This morning, drum-talk speaks of violence.
Taut goatskins erupt in jagged hard rhythms,
like thunder shocks circling in a monsoon storm.

Shouts. Then angry voices. A gunshot.

I am seven years old,
the only white child in a class
known by number, not name.
Number forty-three in a class of forty-three.

Mother Superior slips through the door.
She whispers to our teacher, another nun.
White wimples and black habits
frame their Black Madonna faces.
Mother Superior leaves.
My classmates whimper.

Two older boys rush into the room,
slam shut green wood shutters,
bar them tight with heavy beams
and bolt the door.
The whitewashed room becomes a hot shadowed cave.

Sunrays filter through chinks in slatted shades,
casting narrow shafts of dusty light
across the desks and crying students.

A tumult of rising voices, women's shrieks,
angry shouts of men and the nonstop hammer of drums,
escalates from the marketplace.
"Children, children. Do not cry.
Be calm," the teacher commands.
"Fighting is only in the marketplace. Here we are safe."

Words do nothing to calm my classmates
who sob and wail, jump up and down and shake,
cover their heads with their hands,
protecting skulls from a falling sky.
Dark eyes grow large and full of fear
as they wail louder and louder.

I am confused. Should I be afraid?
Should I sob and wail and cover my head?
What should I do?
I cannot panic like my friends,
though their rising terror soon
penetrates my cool exterior.
In sympathy, my chin quivers.
Tears squeeze from my eyes
but I cannot wail like them.
Little English girls do not wail.
I manage only a choked sob.
The Black Madonna comes to my side:
"Do not worry. This is not for you to worry.
Riot is not against you. Riot is between tribes.
Your mummy will fetch you."

I am helpless among schoolmates
who hold nothing back
with their uninhibited expression of terror.
I am powerless, overwhelmed by the chaos
although I'm told the riots are not against me.
I cannot block the surrounding fear.
But still, I cannot wail like them.
I love my classmates. They accept me
despite my alien skin but I am different
in many more ways than I can understand.

Two weeks before,
parents anxious to challenge a precocious brain,
moved me from a small white class
to this room's 'fast learner' lessons.
Older white children were
long ago abandoned to boarding school.

As number forty-three,
eager to make forty-two new friends.
I joked, played and giggled with them.
They accepted me easily.
I talked in class, added sums wrong,
often paid no attention to the nuns.

The first week, after an arithmetic lesson,
the teacher ordered students
who flunked too many additions
to approach the front of the room.
I filed forward with the group.

As I came near the nun,
alarm flashed in her Black Madonna eyes.
"No, no. You go sit down."
Why did she tell me to return to my desk?
Why was the teacher afraid?
I flunked the same sums as my new friends.
I deserved the punishment as much as them.
I retreated to my seat.

My math-challenged friends suffered cruelly
for their inability with numbers,
the nun's punishment-stick laying heavy lines
across outstretched palms
before they returned to their desks
howling in pain.
Tears for my friends stung my eyes.

Two days later,
we chatted and whispered loudly
as chalk scratched the blackboard.
The nun spun around demanding 'culprits of mischief'
come to the front of the class.
Again I started forward with co-conspirators,
and again, sent back to my desk.

My friends were ordered to hold their ear lobes
while doing fifty knee-squats as we watched.
Bravely, they endured the task,
tears running rivers down their cheeks
before stumbling back to their desks.
Why them, not me?

Number forty-three was special
in the eyes of the Black Madonna.
It was fear of trouble from colonial authorities
that stayed her physical abuse of a little white girl.

I could have taken advantage of the situation
and acted out as much as I wanted.
Instead I became a 'good girl'.
I made sure my sums were correct. I didn't talk in class.
The punishment of returning unpunished to my desk
felt worse than any physical pain my friends would suffer.

The only way to align with other students
was to avoid special treatment.
I kept quiet and behaved.

And now, with chaos
echoing from the marketplace,
in the shuttered classroom of howling children,
again, I am different.
I stay seated at my desk
while friends mill around, crying,
hands still protecting their heads.
The riots so far removed
from anything I have ever known,
I am too afraid to stand up,
run around and wail.
I cannot let fly my own inner chaos.

Before long my mother arrives
and whisks me to the cool, quiet safety of home,

but results of the riot have reached there too.
Our cook from a southern tribe
returns from his daily visit to the market place,
blood dripping down face and shirt from a blow to the head.
I am sent to boarding school in England.
For nine years.

☼☼☼

## 4. The House That Shook And The Ants That Flew

SOMETIMES, coaxing memories feels like hand-cranking an engine to life on wintry days, as grandpa did with his boxy old black car. After a breakfast of black pudding and bacon cooked on a coke-burning stove, he headed to the driveway dressed in a wool jumper, leather-patched at the elbows.

With cold hands, and red face, he cranked the handle on the front grille of the sedan faster and faster till the engine whirred and coughed, and then, like magic, the motor spluttered and came alive. And like that, with a little coaxing, memories arise now of my grandparents' home in London in the years following World War II.

Until I was two, my parents, brother and I shared my grandparents' semi-detached suburban home. For the next four years, my family lived on the Rock of Gibraltar. In the years that followed, when my brother and I didn't fly to Africa for vacations, we often stayed with our grandparents in North London.

My upstairs bedroom overlooked the backyard and railway lines. Nightly, the brick two-story house rattled and shook from passing trains headed north from London, through the suburbs, through the Midlands and beyond, all the way to Scotland. I never made it to Scotland, but perhaps knowing those trains carried people to faraway places nurtured first sparks of curiosity later igniting a love of travel. Even then I must have guessed there was a freedom in traveling to the unknown.

The shaking house and sounds from the rail lines comforted me: whistles, hoots, the CHOO-choo-choo-choo, CHOO-choo-choo-choo of steam engines; the bells and clang of a nearby railway crossing; and always the shudder of the house in response to vibrations of a passing train. If a night suddenly became silent I'd have thought the world had come to an end.

Around six o'clock each evening, the express Royal Scotsman thundered past, speeding on its non-stop journey from London to Edinburgh. Hearing the whistle of the approaching train, my brother and I raced to the end of the yard, climbed onto the wire fence separating our yard from embankment allotments and waved to the passengers zipping past. Less than ten seconds and the Royal Scotsman disappeared in the distance. Other slow trains with chuffing, puffing engines billowed clouds of sooty smoke as they plied the local tracks. In nearby rail yards, engines shunted box cars back and forth between sidings, brakes screeched on the metal rails, box cars slammed into couplings.

When childhood friends visited, the rail lines were a main attraction. Who would dare to perch longest on the wire fence before a metal monster bore down upon us? Slow belching dragons rumbled and swayed down the track, preparing to lunge at their prey of excited children. We raced, squealing, back through the garden, away from the approaching giants.

It had not always been so peaceful by the railway.

Near the end of the war a German bomber heading north missed its target, backtracked following the rail lines, carelessly unloaded its cargo of bombs before fleeing, missing the tracks entirely, making a direct hit at the end of the garden. My grandparents dove under the bunker of their sturdy kitchen table as all the glass and crockery in the house shattered from the force of the blast. I remember willow-pattern dinnerware with every plate stapled and glued together perfectly. The bomb left a ten-foot-wide crater.

Inside the house, at the foot of the stairs by the front door, a grandfather clock chimed each quarter hour from its corner watching over the front hall, benevolent and reassuring with its rhythmic tick-tock and resonant chime. The hallway was filled with possibility. Doors led to the outside world, the dining room (which doubled as an informal sitting room), the more formal back sitting room, the kitchen, and the hidden world of a closet beneath a staircase. Each room had an ambiance unique to its environment. If one ascribed countries to each of the spaces, the formal sitting room was eclectic English country with Chinese touches (grandpa was born in Shanghai). The dining room was casual French, with a wooden table and an open fireplace; the kitchen, Italian with a well-stocked marble-shelved larder of fresh and canned goods. The hall closet (a hide-and-seek favorite) was as darkly mysterious as an unexplored country, with a box of gas masks and wartime paraphernalia left from Grandpa's time in the home guard. The hallway, a neutral zone, witnessed family comings and goings with choices of which country to enter, a staircase to the upper floor, a place to welcome visitors, or leave for the outside world after grabbing an umbrella from the umbrella stand by the front door.

Grandma reigned over a world of bright flowers and flowerbeds. Clematis and morning glory vines climbed trellises by the front porch, next to a deep-blue hydrangea bush, the color enhanced by the yearly burial of rusty iron nails. Roses lined the walkway to the front gate. Delphiniums, love-in-the mist, asters, dahlias, marigolds, pansies, chrysanthemums, Chinese lanterns, yarrow, alyssum and flowering groundcover, grew in flower beds along neighboring fences in the back yard. I'm sure there must have been snow drops, daffodils and tulips out there somewhere too.

Grandpa's garden world included the lawn, vegetable garden, and fruit trees. A laburnum tree grew from a small island in the lawn, showering a rain of golden blossoms in summer, followed by handfuls of red berries in the fall. At the back of the vegetable garden, next to the bomb crater, he tended a small orchard of pear trees, four types of apple trees, and two plum trees. Between the fruit trees and the vegetables, rows of blackberries, raspberries, gooseberries, red currants, black currants and strawberries delivered a rich harvest of berries for canning, jams, birds, and for my juice stained lips. Cabbages, cauliflower, potatoes, onions, carrots, parsnips, lettuce and radishes were the staple vegetables.

As a result of loving care throughout wartime, this wealth of nature flourished in the small suburban back garden in north London, despite the rude interruption of the bomb. With grandpa's work, the crater became a large, rich and fertile compost pile enhanced by weekly gifts left on the street by the local rag-and-bone-man's horse. On the embankment between the garden fence and the rail lines the land had been divided into allotments for people who had no land for a garden or chicken coop, providing much needed nourishment in a time of food scarcity and war time rationing.

Helping grandma weed the flower beds was a favorite chore. Each summer, I dug slate stepping stones out of the lawn, hacking away at greedy grass to prevent the stones from yielding to an encroaching mat of green. I watched fascinated as ants under the stones scurried from the sudden light, dragging their food and eggs to safety along a maze of intricate passageways. One hot day each summer, usually the hottest day of the year, the air filled with clouds of flying ants.

Birds flew through the yard; sparrows, robins, black birds and starlings the most frequent visitors, and with abundant fruit and berries in summer and fall, the birds were never hungry. A metal bird bath in the shape of a hollow duck held court on a low wall separating a small terrace from the main garden. The bird bath, sculpted in China, had been brought to England by my great grandfather who was a silk merchant in Shanghai.

Now, on the internet, I find a photo of the front of the house, the front garden changed, half paved over for a second parking space. I wonder if the backyard is still as wondrous and plentiful as I remember it, and I hope that if children live in the house now, they enjoy it as much as I did as a child.

And I wonder too if the house still shudders at night and if the ants still fly in summer.

# 5. The Servant Warrior

"BOY!" my father roars, through cheeks etched by veins of drink and the hot African sun. "These eggs no hot! Toast burned! Take away!" At nine in the morning, sweat already beads his bald head.

Overhead, the ceiling fan whirs with a low hum, spreading the familiar scent of burned toast throughout the bungalow.

I cringe. Though I have never been the target of my father's rage, the threat of its unpredictable force often ruins my day. The vehemence of his shouting spoils breakfast far more than any culinary disaster. I don't mind eating lukewarm eggs from the scrawny chickens that peck the red dirt of our dusty compound, and I actually like burned toast.

My older brother, Christopher, glances at me and conceals a smirk, while my mother keeps her eyes lowered. Ali, the target of my father's rage, takes it all in stride. He doesn't flinch or reveal emotion. My heart goes out to him.

"Yes Suh," Ali responds softly as the plates vanish from the breakfast table in a flash, his deft hands balancing the offending plates like a pro.

However much my father shouts, grumbles and complains, Ali delivers his often-thankless work with skill and equanimity.

THIS scene repeated itself in one form or another for most of my childhood years in Northern Nigeria when I wasn't at boarding school or with my grandparents in England. The more I felt ashamed of my father's behavior, the more my admiration and compassion for Ali grew.

For nine years Ali faithfully served our family as 'head boy' in charge of a team of 'small boy', cook, and gardener. When my family first set up house in Kaduna, Northern Nigeria, Ali arrived on our doorstep from a tribal village of Hausa horsemen warriors, from deep in the bush up north at the edge of the Sahara, offering to serve our family needs with integrity and skill. For nine years he ran our household with patience, pride, humility, and natural ease. If there were mistakes, he quickly made amends. Dignity and loyalty personified, Ali was a peaceful warrior who stood a head above us all. Even as a servant, in a uniform stiff with starch, he emanated royalty. For nine years, I loved Ali.

He was everything my father was not. My father smelled of bitter pipe tobacco, sweat and alcohol. Ali's scent spoke of the mystery of the desert at dawn, mixed with spices, sweetness and dust. Tall and spare, barefoot and wide-toed, he moved with the grace of a gazelle with space flowing between his bones. He wasn't like the other servants. His skin didn't shine the color of tar; he didn't smell like the cook from the jungle down south whose stained Swiss-cheese t-shirt clung to a back dripping with sweat. Ali's smooth skin was the color of chocolate blended with milk and almonds.

On days off, as chief of his other household, Ali donned creamy tribal robes, all billows and softness, with a wreath of turban piled wide above his head. He sailed away from the compound on his bicycle, like a Spanish galleon, with an elegant wife balanced on the handlebars. I liked Ali like that. He was husband to not only one, but four wives who grinned often through betel-stained teeth, and he was father to a flock of children who giggled, chuckled and squealed and never wore shoes. I longed to belong to his family. I would sneak out to the servants' compound to visit their red-mud smoky rooms and play with his children under the hibiscus, paw-paw and sweet-scented frangipani trees.

21

When Ali babysat Christopher and me on summer evenings and electricity failed at the height of a monsoon storm, he would light the kerosene lantern on the verandah and stand silently out of sight but nearby, a protective shadow, while we played cards or board games until we fell asleep (or pretended to). He carried us to our beds, then lay on his rush sleeping-mat outside the door, guarding us, awaiting the return of our parents from the frequent party or social event of the week. I snuggled under cool sheets and soon slept in a cocoon of safety and protection, knowing Ali watched over us.

The following morning I would squat beside the French doors to the verandah, chin resting on my fists, and watch the elegant rhythmic swoop and swing of Ali's twig brush as he swept away piles of moths and bugs that had flown too close to the lantern flame.

Ali saved my life. Twice. During a birthday party, a puff adder slithered close and threatened death as my friends and I played in high grass. Within seconds of my sudden screams, a slice of his machete restored safety to the world. Another time, when a scorpion crawled from a length of pipe I held in my hands, he grabbed the pipe and smashed the treacherous insect with a rock. And Ali frequently delighted me when, with the stealth and awareness of a hunter, he clapped his hands mid-air, never failing to squish a mean-faced African hornet between deep-lined palms calloused by drudgery, then grinned in my direction as he flicked away the now harmless creature.

Protecting and caring for me like neither my father nor mother, our relationship was a quiet, simple and innocent heart connection, although I don't remember ever having a conversation with him. My love for him was not confused by wants, needs, expectations, rules, emotions (or lack of), and land mines of 'love', as in 'parental'.

Ali shone with traits my father lacked and, maybe as a result of this, Ali's mildness, poise and composure wore at a nerve inside my father, infuriating him. My father was an atheist, and perhaps disliked Ali most of all when, at dawn, morning, afternoon, evening, and at night, Ali unrolled his mat for prayers, bowed down and gave his life to Allah.

When I returned to Africa for the last time in my sixteenth summer, I was surprised when Ali wasn't standing tall in his usual place next to zinnia-filled pots on the verandah steps, waiting to greet me with a wide smile. When I asked my mother what had happened to him, she told me he had 'gone bush, up north' in February with his wives and children. Before leaving, Ali warned her that a juju man had placed a curse on the house and family and he said he did not want his own family to suffer with ours. My mother could not persuade him to stay.

Ali was right about the curse. On April Fools' Day that year my brother ended his life by taking cyanide. I never saw Ali again, and will never know whether he played any part in the curse. It was also the last year I saw my parents together.

That last African summer I sat alone for hours on the deserted verandah and played the Ray Charles song "Born to Lose" over and over on the old record player till grooves in the vinyl were scratched and worn. Christopher had flown too close to the lantern flame and Ali was not there to sweep aside the sorrow left behind. The house hung low with grief and the summer heat weighed heavy as my mother and father walked dazed, silent and tight-lipped through the ashes of their African life.

Years later, on a trip to India in search of 'enlightenment', I rented a small mud-walled room in the servants' compound of an old colonial house, reminiscent of servants' rooms at our Kaduna home. The following week, I bowed down, took initiation and offered my heart at the feet of a mystic holy man who wore creamy billowing robes and whose skin was the color of chocolate blended with milk and almonds.

# 6. Philosophy

WHY did I enjoy reading—or rather skimming— often incomprehensible densely rich philosophical works of fiction or non-fiction? Why did those books appeal to me at some level? Even though many times I re-read words, sentences and paragraphs of profound ideological insight, my brain resisted intellectual comprehension. But when I ceased my struggle to understand, I sensed the mood behind the writing, the elevated atmosphere, the matrix from which those ideas were birthed. In a process of transmutation, the author's state of being behind the words had been injected into the sentences, affecting the flow and the hidden nuance of the writing itself, which I instinctively received, despite whether I made an ounce of sense of the scholarly meaning of the language. Turned on by the vibration behind the writing, I was touched by the author's presence subtly radiating through even the weightiest subjects.

Of course, this wasn't always the case; some tomes, arid as a late summer ditch, were quickly recycled after a minimal skim. For me it was always about whether the sub-text of the author behind the language shone through.

While it is much easier to sit and listen to someone lecture in a melodic voice, there is pleasure in surrendering to written words that hum with underlying beauty and harmonic overtones, even if not understood. I long to lose myself in the fluid poetry of written words, and disappear through the enchantment of a resonant voice.

The first storyteller in my life, my grandfather, was born in Shanghai, the son of a silk merchant. As a young child, snuggled safe under a warm eiderdown, I listened spellbound to his slow resonant voice, wise and seemingly ancient, as he led me on imaginative journeys across foreign lands and oceans, spinning tales of ships loaded with exotic cargo as they sailed south Asian seas with the ever-present danger of piracy. The adventure stories, though not philosophical, were tinged with excitement, foreign, strange and elusive, inspiring my young imagination with both a thirst for mysteries of the unknown and the subtle energies behind the sharing of language.

In school I probably learned more about life by reading novels in the school library than from any of my teachers. I remember no teacher or textbook inspiring me with their use of words.

While on vacation in southern Spain, at the age of nineteen, I met a Professor of Moral Philosophy from New York City University. He was tall, blonde, and tanned, not the picture you'd expect of a university professor. Looking back, I wonder what he saw in me—I definitely couldn't keep up with his friends, a smart hip crowd of ex-pat 'beautiful people'. Maybe it was my long hair, moves on the dance floor and my English innocence that attracted him. We smoked kief, listened to Nina Simone and old blues records with Lars and Lilimoo, Swedish ex-pat artists, in a sun-filled whitewashed villa overlooking the Mediterranean.

The professor whisked me away to Morocco, an even more exotic location, where we smoked more kief—a lot of kief—consumed hash candy and drank mint tea. Afternoons, we wandered vast deserted beaches outside Tangier where fierce Atlantic winds tirelessly scoured a fine haze of sand across miles of dunes. I sat cross-legged and listened, spellbound, without understanding, as he talked philosophy for hours. I was enthralled in the presence of this man whose words sang and wooed and wowed me with their American/Irish accent (he was originally from Ireland). Here was a man who had captained yachts for International Ocean races (I later sailed with him); who had written a book called "Scarcity and Evil"; who knew his way around the world. I don't remember a word he said. I floated on the mental energy behind the words. My whole being thirsted for intellectual nourishment, though if he had asked me to repeat back to him even the smallest portion of what he'd said, I would have had to remain silent. Even to this day, it is the feeling of pleasurable awe that I remember from those timeless moments sitting on a Moroccan beach listening to his voice and eloquent words that rang in harmony with the brilliant blue sky, the blowing sand and the persistent wind.

Years later, in India, for hours each morning, I again sat cross-legged, enthralled, listening to discourses given by a guru who had begun his career as a Professor of Philosophy. Again, if someone had questioned me about the substance of his words, I would not have been able to respond coherently. It was the state of no-mind beyond the words that held me captive. Philosophy was the music dancing in the silence, delivered seamlessly in a hypnotic voice with deep resonance, while bypassing the intellect entirely. Each month he alternated discourses in English, and then Hindi. Despite the familiarity of listening to his words in English, the Hindi discourses allowed me to sink deeper into the mystery of sound beyond words, all the while knowing the sound was charged with the depths of insight and understanding.

Even though I seldom read complex philosophical or esoteric literature any more, I have never lost a sense of wonderment at nourishment offered through insightful intelligence beyond the intellect, whether I understand the words or not, whether written or spoken—the authentic energetic wisdom of gifts of heart/mind words.

# 7. Seeking Creative Work

AFTER delivering the classified ad to the English-language newspaper office in downtown Athens, I take the last change out of my pocket to pay for a bus ride back to the hillside apartment overlooking the Hilton, shared with two friends. Then I wait, confident someone will respond to my words: 'English girl with secretarial skills seeks creative work.'

Another town, another adventure. I wonder how, time after time, with minimum forethought or planning, I land on my feet. Life is good. I have my health, youth, friends, and most of all, freedom, but money is scarce. I only had enough bus fare to visit the newspaper. Not a big deal. After having to leave my English teaching job on the island of Evia, I am hopeful the search for rent money will soon bear fruit. I'll get by; English speakers do. Wealthy Athenians pay well for private English lessons for their children. But I don't only want to teach English; I'm open to trying something different, even if I don't know what. Which is why I worded my ad the way I did.

I HADN'T planned on staying on in Greece after my vacation the previous summer. The thought had never crossed my mind to become an English language teacher. The job materialized unexpectedly when an Englishman approached me while I waited in line for mail outside American Express in Athens. The man, Clive, introduced himself and asked if I, too, was English. He would soon be leaving Greece, and the language school where he'd taught on Evia needed a replacement English teacher—specifically someone from England. Without thinking, I agreed to visit the school the next day even though I had no teaching experience, had no idea how to teach, didn't speak Greek, and had a ride back to England two days later. Clive reassured me all I would have to do was stand in front of the class and speak English—the rest would happen on its own.

That evening, my head spun with romantic ideas of how I would spend all my spare time writing when I wasn't teaching. Wasn't that what beginning writers and poets did—escape to isolated exotic locations so they could let words flow unimpeded, with no distractions other than good friends and a bottle of wine. Wasn't that the life poet Leonard Cohen enjoyed right then, in that same country? Anything was better than the threat of an endless dreary existence under grey British skies offering zero inspiration for an aspiring young writer such as me—it was a nice dream for my last two days in Greece. How could I say no to a fun side trip with a fellow countryman who had lived there for a while, regardless of the result of the interview?

Surprisingly, despite my lack of experience, the language school offered me the job and lined up a work permit. After a short trip back to London to sublet my apartment, I returned to the island of Evia and began teaching. But it was not as simple as Clive had promised. I was not naturally an extrovert, after growing up with warnings to: 'be seen and not heard,' 'speak only when spoken to' and even harsher, to 'keep my mouth shut.' I struggled through long afternoons standing in front of young children who understood almost nothing of what I said, and who spoke in a language I did not understand. I wished I had learned more Greek. While on vacation I had picked up only minimal social greetings, essential food vocabulary, plus a couple of swear words I understood but had never used.

As soon as I began teaching, I knew I wasn't cut out to stand in front of a classroom, or an audience of any kind. Even though I liked the young students, and they liked me, however well I prepared lessons, I dreaded being the center of attention with all eyes watching me, and all ears straining to understand my words. I dreaded, even more, times when I wasn't the center of attention, powerless and ineffective when chatter, giggles, foot shuffling and passing of notes hovered on the brink of classroom chaos.

My fantasies of an imagined writing life faded fast. Faced with the reality of being the only native English speaker in the small town of Chalcis, my intentions and enthusiasm plummeted. I had left hip late 1960s London for Evia and landed in a time warp. The majority of the population had never ventured beyond a twenty-mile radius; donkeys and chickens roamed the dusty streets; life continued much the same as it had for the last five hundred years. I had rented a room in a rundown house owned by two ancient sisters who wore faded black dresses and spoke no English. Frustrated by failed efforts at communication, I pointed to words in a dictionary. When the toothless crones grinned and shook their heads, I realized neither of them knew how to read or write. I felt desperately alone.

At night, I sat on my narrow bed with a pen and writing pad balanced on my knees, ready and determined to begin the 'writing life,' but nothing came, apart from feeble attempts to describe the solace I found in 'loukoumades,' a mouth-watering Greek honey-puff dessert dripping with sweetness. I had envisioned the adventure and rewards of a free-flowing writing life—but the writing life turned out to be nothing but hard, frustrating work with negligible results. Was it possible I had escaped a future grey dreary existence in England only to be confronted with the dreary ordinariness of my own being? What happened to the promise of fun, adventure and excitement of living in a foreign country? Where were the good friends and a bottle of wine?

The fates were kind to me though, in a roundabout way. I soon learned misfortune can lead to interesting new circumstances.

Clive, the previous teacher, returned to Evia briefly to check on a house being built on land he'd purchased. He invited me, on my day off from school, to visit his property. The day turned out to be an iconic Greek blue-sky day where white-washed houses overlooked deserted sandy coves and sun-rays flashed sparkles across a turquoise sea. The view from Clive's property fit the idyllic description perfectly. My heart began to expand with joy, a blissful feeling I had almost forgotten after so many depressing days. At last, this was the Greece of my dreams.

Then I stepped on a rusty nail.

The nail spiked clear through my thin rubber sandal into the sole of my foot. I cried out in pain, but held off with my small vocabulary of Greek swear words in the presence of the construction workers. The wound was superficial, nothing serious, but the workmen, after gestures and excited words translated by Clive, beat my foot with a wooden board to make the blood flow, then insisted I go to the local hospital for a tetanus shot. Which I did.

Later that afternoon, feeling wounded and woozy, I attended a 'name day' celebration, the Greek equivalent of a birthday party, for a student from my school. One of the other guests, a Greek man I hadn't noticed before in the small town, walked over and introduced himself in English with a perfect American accent, "Hi, I'm Tomas—call me Tom. I've seen you around."

"Wow, you speak great English. Have you been to America?"

He laughed. "I am American. I look Greek with my dark hair and complexion. All four of my grandparents emigrated to the US."

"So what are you doing here?"

"Same as you, teaching English. At your rival language institute. I've heard all about you. The headmaster of my school is insanely jealous your school hired an English teacher from England."

"So I'm not the only foreigner in town!"

"Are you OK? It looks like you're breaking out with something."

I told him about my earlier puncture-by-rusty-nail and tetanus shot ordeal. Beginning to feel feverish, I headed to the bathroom and looked in a mirror, barely recognizing a rapidly swelling face and rash-speckled arms. Tom led me into the garden, lit a joint, handed it to me and pulled a small flask of whiskey from his back pocket.

"You look like you could use this."

"You're right. Thank you. You've no idea what a relief it is to meet someone who speaks English! And who offers me a drink and a joint! Especially when I'm beginning to look like a space alien."

"I'm taking you back to the hospital."

I spent the night at the hospital, feeling like a pin cushion after further needle punctures reversed the tetanus shot reaction.

After that fortunate/unfortunate/fortunate day, Tom and I met regularly, wandering through the town arm-in-arm, at the market, and at a waterfront park overlooking the small harbor where families gathered on Sundays for their weekly promenade. We did not hide our open affection. Soon, whispered rumors crept through the narrow streets—the two English teachers were more than friends.

Perhaps it was my too-short skirts, the scandalous friendship of unmarried foreign teachers, or just the malicious gossip of old women that contributed to the building ire of Tom's headmaster, who already resented my position as a teacher at his rival's school. He wanted me run out of town. Within a month, police knocked at the door of my school demanding the headmaster produce my English teaching credentials, even though my work permit was in order. No degree, no special certificate—no teaching job. There was nothing my headmaster could do to persuade the police I was more than qualified to teach English; after all, I was an English speaker from England.

How naïve I had been about teaching and small town Greek life. And my desire to write. I was happy to lose the teaching job; disappointed to fail my writing dream; and sad to leave my growing friendship with Tom although I knew I would still see him after I moved to Athens to share an apartment with a couple of friends, also English teachers. He was welcome to visit whenever he could. He taught four days a week, so on long weekends we had time to explore Greece. I enjoyed his confidence and easy-going company, exploring and traveling to hidden beaches, snorkeling and camping from an old red VW van we'd painted with a giant white octopus. Though I was fond of Tom, I wouldn't have said I was in love.

THE day after placing my ad, I await the phone call that will decide my future, hopefully with an offer of a decent income, even if temporary. I walk around and around the spacious white apartment, the rooms empty except for rush mats on the wooden floors, my sleeping bag, and those of my two friends. The warm smell of fresh baked bread floats up from the downstairs bakery. I water pot plants growing on the balcony, roll a joint and take a couple of hits. Lying on my sleeping bag on the floor, I float to where I picture how my perfect job might be, but what comes to mind is more a description of what I don't want it to be.

Anything but work in an office, anything other than nine-to-five drudgery. Why had I put the word 'secretarial' in my ad? At least I said 'creative work'. But the two don't fit together. There's nothing creative about secretarial work. But I didn't want to write only 'creative work,' opening the door to any wild interpretation that might not offer anything I could reasonably consider. What do I have in mind? Not much. Travel? I love to travel, but I want to stay in Greece. I enjoy exploring Greece. Maybe something will manifest to build my writing skills, though I honestly realize now I don't have any writing skills. I decide to accept any work described as 'other than repetitive and boring.' Although maybe I'll draw the line at serving drunken Greeks or tourists in a bar.

What I'm doing at the moment feels like the perfect job: lying on the floor with a shaft of sunlight falling across my body; listening to distant sounds of the city; breathing the aroma of fresh baked bread. But who would pay me to do that? More realistically, I think the perfect job might involve travel, writing, lying on a warm sandy beach under a striped umbrella listening to wavelets ripple against the shore. Well, that isn't exactly realistic either. I sigh.

The phone rings.

"Hello, this is Lynda."

"My name is Stavros," says a mellow Greek voice. "I saw your ad. I'm looking for someone to help type letters to companies in England. My written English is not so good. Would you like to come to my office for a talk?"

Trying to hide my reluctance, I hesitate, then answer, "Yes," and ask what time we should meet.

"Four o'clock this afternoon?" He gives me an address downtown.

"I'll be there."

I groan inwardly. Secretarial. Typing letters. I can't get away from it. So much for 'creative'. But I need the money. Perhaps there will be other phone calls. But what if there aren't?

I borrow bus fare from my flat mates, an Australian and his American girlfriend. I dress in my most conservative clothes and head downtown.

I find the office on a shady side street, walk through the unmarked door and step down into an unassuming room with two wooden desks and a filing cabinet in one corner. On one of the desks is an old typewriter. A Greek man, I guess in his early forties, sits behind the other desk. He stands, looks up at me, smiles and shakes my hand firmly. He's at least five inches shorter than me, casually dressed in a cable-knit fisherman sweater and dark jeans. Black curly hair, shiny dark eyes, squat, slightly plump; he doesn't look like a typical businessman.

"Stavros, Stavros Mavro-Mikailis. Some people call me Black Michael. You can call me that if you like. Pleased to meet you, Miss Lynda."

I glance around the office walls: an old map of Greece; a faded photograph of a distinguished man wearing an official uniform well-decorated with medals and ribbons; a photograph of a yacht with a speed boat tied up alongside.

Stavros watches me looking at the photos. "A relative. And the family yacht."

I smile my friendliest smile. "I like the name Stavros." The name Black Michael doesn't quite fit. Whatever the job is, if he hires me, I think I could at least handle it for a couple of weeks so I'll have cash in my pocket while waiting for another creative possibility to manifest. The place and the man feel innocuous enough.

"Shall we begin with typing a letter, to check typing skills?" He motions me to the desk with the typewriter. "I import components for construction machinery from English companies. I need help with correspondence. I'm sorry, it's not, how do you say—exciting." He places a hand-written letter on the desk. "Please type and make corrections to my English."

While I type, Stavros leans back in his chair at the other desk watching me, but I don't feel nervous. The man seems decent and friendly. The letter is simple and quick to type, with several easily-remedied grammatical and language errors. I hand him the letter. He glances over it briefly. "Very good," he says, then adds, "Tell me about yourself."

At ease, knowing I've done well with my typing test, I share what I think he'd like to hear. I carefully edit some of my less-than-conservative past, but tell him how I had to leave my English teaching job in Chalcis because of my boyfriend's jealous headmaster.

He smiles. "Yes, there are some Greeks like that."

I add I'd like to be a writer one day.

He nods in appreciation. He asks me what I think of Greece and what I've seen of the country. I reply how I love the islands I've visited, the ancient sites, Greek food, the climate, and the people. I leave out how narrow-minded I found most small town people, especially when I understood enough Greek to know what they were saying about me when they thought I couldn't understand. Stavros seems happy.

"You have the job if you like. A few hours a week. And I'll pay you well. Come next Monday morning, ten o'clock."

"Thank you. That would be good. I'll be here." Yes, I think, not bad work for a week or two. I get up to leave.

"Wait." Stavros pauses, looking directly at me, "I did not tell you the truth about the position. I wanted first to see who you are, if you are right for the real job I have."

Puzzled, I sit down again, wondering what he'll say.

"For a long time, I wanted to publish a tourist guide to Greece written by two people. The book will be written from a Greek man, as well as Greece from a foreign woman. I prefer the foreign woman to be from England."

I can hardly believe it. What an opportunity! My ad is going to pay off, and not only with cash. What was it I'd dreamed of earlier when I lay on the floor of my apartment? My dream come true! Travel. Exploration. Writing.

"That sounds wonderful," I say as evenly as I can, trying to hide my excitement. Then I wonder if there's a hidden agenda, although he seems docile and friendly. He has, however, lied to me about typing letters. Maybe the job includes that too; perhaps the travel book is only wishful thinking.

"I've already begun working on how it can be. I have many photographs to show you, Lynda, back at my apartment— photos of beautiful islands I want to visit again, with a foreigner. I live close to here on the top floor of a building with the best view over the Acropolis and city. Would you like to visit? Are you busy now? We could eat souvlaki on the way there."

I feel I cannot say no. I feel comfortable enough around him, and if this man Stavros makes unwanted moves, I can tell him I live with my boyfriend and I told him where I was going. Not true, but it might protect me. If the man's ideas are real, if he's telling the truth and already has photographs for a guidebook, working with him could be a once-in-a-lifetime chance to learn writing skills, plus visit amazing places. Beginning with seeing the best view in Athens overlooking the Acropolis.

"Yes, I'd like that."

When we step out onto the sidewalk, sounds of the hot daytime city have quieted. Beeping horns and the roar and screech of traffic no longer echo through the streets and alleys. My prospective employer and I sit at a table outside a small neighborhood café eating souvlaki, while haunting bouzouki melodies drift from a nearby jukebox. Magenta bougainvillea blossoms scent the air with honeysuckle sweetness from a trellis strung with many-colored lights. Dusk fades to evening. Lulled by the pleasant atmosphere, I keep my many questions to myself, while Stavros chats amiably about idyllic destinations he would like to show me.

We walk a short distance through town until he stops in front of a high-rise office tower. "This is it. I live here. I own the penthouse."

I hide my surprise. How can he afford a penthouse!

"I know what you think. How can I live in such a place when I have only a small import business?"

"No, not at all!" I say, wondering if he can read my mind.

"My grandfather was a famous colonel, big in the government. That is his photo on the wall of my office. I come from a powerful family."

Satisfied with his explanation, I congratulate myself on my good luck, and all from a small ad in a newspaper.

The penthouse is luxurious. I gasp when I see the spectacular view. Floor-to-ceiling plate glass windows look out over a panorama of the Acropolis and Parthenon, fully lit at night. Stavros waits in silence while I look around the room. Hanging on the living room walls are large National Geographic-quality photographs of Greek coast lines, islands at sunset, and underwater shots of submerged ruins and colorful fish. A glass case holds a remarkable collection of perfect seashells, large and small.

38

Stavros watches my wide-eyed wonder. "Some things I like to do: dive, take photos, collect shells."

Another glass case contains Greek vases, some chipped and faded, some flawlessly painted with traditional patterns and figures. "Greece has much ancient history," he says as he pulls out a smaller glass-covered jewelry case from under a desk and sets it on a table. "These are all antique coins."

Some of the encrusted coins look like they've been lying on the ocean floor for centuries.

"Would you like a glass of wine? We can talk about the book."

"Yes. Thank you." I guess it won't be the cheap retsina I usually drink.

He hands me a glass of wine. We sink onto a soft dark leather couch looking out over the view of the Acropolis. "Yamas! To our joint venture!" he toasts, then grows quiet, a serious look darkening his face.

Now I begin to feel uncomfortable. I don't find him even the least physically attractive. Is this where he's going to make advances?

"Lynda, you remember in my office when I told you typing letters wasn't the real job I was interviewing you for? Well, the tourist guidebook is—and isn't—the real job either. I wanted to see if I can trust you and if we get along. I think you are perfect for what I have in mind." His look lightens.

I wonder what's coming next.

"I already told you I like to dive. I also collect antiques. I know places underwater no one knows, places where submerged ruins hide many valuable artifacts. I know where sunken ships are undiscovered, on the ocean floor, shipwrecks from rocks off the islands. Many wrecks never found, sailing ships carrying treasure across the Mediterranean."

This is beginning to sound like an adventure movie.

"When I go to England for my import business I sometimes carry one or two small pieces and sell them to a dealer in London."

Smuggling. So this is what this is about. Still, I keep quiet; I wait to hear what he has to say.

"The government recently won't allow anyone to take antiques out of the country. I love my country—my grandfather was a powerful man here, and I love the ancient artifacts. But I know most of the valuable and beautiful objects will never be seen, only hidden on shelves in the basement of a museum in Greece to gather dust. That is a shame. So why not let collectors in other countries share the glorious past of Greece around the world?"

"But isn't it risky and illegal?"

"I own the fastest power boat in Greece. The coast guard can never catch me if I take anything from an underwater wreck or ruin. And I have powerful friends in high political places. But to be safe, I need the cover story of the guide book, which is where I think of you."

He smiles, raises an eyebrow and nods at me. "No one suspects a couple traveling in the Greek islands, anchored in secret coves, gathering book material—we would write a newspaper article saying what we are doing. And yes, we would write a book. With my boat I'll take you to the most beautiful places no one knows about."

I weigh his words. It's true it doesn't sound too risky. Plus, a chance to see amazing locations, with a little excitement thrown in. What an adventure it could be!

"There's another part of the job. Sometimes I would ask you to carry small easy-to-hide items out of the country. It is not dangerous. You are from England. No one questions an innocent English girl who goes home to visit parents. You will be well paid. Plus you have plenty of time to write—both the guide book and your own work. You could save money too. Better than working in an office, no?"

I am almost convinced.

He gets up and opens the case with his coin collection. "See this one coin. It is over two thousand years old. Worth thousands of pounds.

"But it is important for people to know we are a couple, even if we are not. When we travel together it is better you do not have a boyfriend. And you cannot tell a single person about what I have told you today, not even a boyfriend, or closest friends."

No, I think. No. Perhaps I can keep a secret, but I'm not willing to give up my growing friendship, and, I now realize, my growing love for Tom. I will not give up Tom. I say nothing.

"Now I am talking seriously." Stavros beckons me over to the desk, slowly slides open a draw and points to a gun. "But I must tell you, if you say a word of what I have told you to anyone, I would not hesitate to use this on a quick trip out to sea."

My knees grow weak, my throat tightens. I have never seen a gun this close before. Guns are illegal in England; even the police don't carry firearms. How am I going to get out of this mess? I don't want anything to do with this man, or his promises of writing a book, money and exotic travel. No wonder he's called Black Michael. He is a liar and a thief. And dangerous. Maybe he's even taken some previous innocent woman 'on a quick trip out to sea'.

I think quickly and try to look calm. I am also a good liar. "Don't worry; I won't say a word to anyone. Not even to my boyfriend. You can trust me."

"Good. So your answer is 'yes' to the job?" He closes the desk drawer.

Afraid my voice will tremble if I speak, I smile and nod to Stavros and slowly pick up my bag.

"So, I'll expect you at my office, ten o'clock on Monday morning."

In the elevator, my knees still shaking, I wonder what the next response to my ad might be; I also think it might be wise to change my phone number.

# 8. New York

IF I hadn't met Harvey, I wouldn't have met Fred. Oh, but this is titled New York isn't it. Okay, I'll begin there.

That fall, a friend headed to New England gave me a ride from Idaho to New York City. In the city I planned to earn money for a ticket to England to visit my mother, and then to Spain to visit my father. Although my friend's destination was Boston, she first dropped me off in Manhattan at her friend John's apartment, assuring me I'd be able to crash there for a couple of nights. John agreed to let me stay, but for only one night, on the floor; there were already three extra people staying with him, one of them a speed freak who slept in the bathtub. That evening, a friend of John's stopped by and after hearing my story kindly offered to rent me his small walk-up apartment on East 5th Street in the East Village for $50 a month. What luck. Harvey lived in a loft downtown, but kept the small apartment for anyone needing a place to stay, and occasionally to meet people in the daytime. Perfect since I planned on working during the day.

The first evening at Harvey's apartment, when I opened the door and switched on the light the walls appeared to be moving—cockroaches scurried to hide behind any appliance and available crack. Would they come back to haunt me when I turned off the lights, all alone in a strange city? I lay awake for a long time nervously awaiting the slightest rustle, eventually pulling the covers tight over my head and falling asleep.

The next day I found a thrift store where I bought work appropriate clothing of a white shirt and black skirt, then signed on with a secretarial agency as a temp. Somehow I managed to pass a typing test and impress the owner with my 'proper' English accent. She hired me and sent me on an assignment starting the following morning with a company computerizing the New York stock exchange.

The company occupied a temporary office of tables and chairs on the top floor of the exchange building. I was the only woman among fourteen men, at a time when women were not yet allowed on the trading floor. After the New York Mets won the World Series in 1969, we crowded around the windows high above Wall Street and watched the ticker tape parade celebrating their win. On coffee breaks, I sat on a table while the men stood around and listened to tales of my life in a hippy community in a ghost town in the mountains of Idaho where I had lived for the previous fourteen months. The tales were well edited, something I've perfected over the years according to my audience—with sufficient spice to energize and entertain, but not too much that might antagonize and shock.

On another assignment I temped at J Walter Thompson, and then briefly for a daytime soap writer who watched the current TV episode while dictating a future one. After saving enough money to cover my fare to Europe, I quit the agency.

Then, set up beside other artists, I sold artwork, prints of my pen and ink mandala coloring wheels on a Manhattan sidewalk, my first experience of street and market vending, something I've enjoyed, and a way of being in the world, that has provided income on and off for years.

In the meantime Harvey and I had become lovers, and I always looked forward to his visits to the funky little apartment in the East Village with the roaming roaches and a bathtub in the kitchen.

I flew back to England and stayed with my mother for the first time since moving to America, then, after a brief disastrous visit to my father in Spain, returned to the States, arriving in New York early in the morning, with nowhere to go. I called Harvey. He said to come on down and stay with him in his loft. Excited to see him, and ready to settle into a relationship for however long it might last, I headed downtown. Was I crazy? He had a Doberman that wasn't housebroken, and I knew he dealt cocaine (I'd found a suitcase under the bed in his apartment on East 5$^{th}$ street). But he was a beautiful gentle man with wild red hair, divorced from his African-American wife, son of a Southern Baptist minister, had been thrown out of WestPoint, and he taught computer programming at City University. A complex man who suited my own complexity and adventurous nature.

So there I was that first evening in Harvey's loft, disoriented from jet lag. I took off my traveling clothes, immediately feeling more at home and comfortable wandering around naked. We dropped acid, the trip quickly becoming everything a good trip should be, riding waves of fear, surge, intensity and bliss, mellow, mind-expanding and hallucinatory at the same time. Then the phone rang. Through a psychedelic haze I heard Harvey tell me a friend would come over to pick up a package. Too far out of it to think of putting on clothes, when the door opened I stayed sitting cross-legged on the bed, stoned out of my head, unable to shift a muscle. Fred walked in. Immediately our eyes locked. I froze, acutely aware of my nakedness but I could not move. But it was the eye contact that blew me away. The eyes. He turned into a Cheshire cat, an ancient wise woman, a demonic half spirit, and then back to Cheshire cat. Waves of color flowed off his body. Energy from third eye to third eye streamed lines of purple lightning with flashes of gold between us. Pow! The most intensely powerful meeting I had ever had. Then he left.

A couple of days later Fred walked toward me as I strolled through Chinatown. Again, those lines flashed between our heads. Too shy to say anything except the simplest of greetings, I kept walking.

Two days later, while Harvey was at his teaching job, I met Fred on the stairs in Harvey's building. He told me he was house-sitting for the painter who lived in the loft below Harvey. That afternoon he knocked on the door and asked to borrow a cup of milk. I was unable to carry on an intelligible conversation, still overwhelmed by the supernatural power of our first meeting.

He came to visit again the next day. Communication was easier, but my boundaries were non-existent after our first meeting and I soon dissolved into the vortex of our energetic mix. We ended up making love. What a mistake. What was I doing! I definitely wasn't thinking. I heard footsteps on the stairs. Harvey! I didn't expect him to come home on his lunch hour. There was no time to hide our guilt. The door opened, he saw us together, guessed what had happened and bristled with a cold quiet rage. I knew he kept a large knife by his bed, and didn't know if the Doberman responded to attack commands. Terrified, I stuffed my clothes into my pack and we headed for the door. We didn't go back. Fred didn't return to his housesit. I was a mess, confused, upset and guilty about betraying Harvey, at the same time completely entranced by Fred, despite him being three inches shorter and several years older than me, resembling an old witch, with a demonic cat-like look I saw even when not on acid. And those purple/gold lines.

We spent several surreal idyllic days crashing on the hard floor of an apartment belonging to a friend of his in Manhattan and wandering in a daze around Chinatown, before picking up a u-drive vehicle to deliver in Los Angeles. When we went to claim his possessions stored in a locker at Grand Central station everything he owned fit in a small briefcase containing his writing, astrology notes and books, plus a small guitar—the essential tools for life as an itinerant astrologer, writer and jazz guitar player. We drove across the country to Southern

46

California where I purchased my first car, a salmon-colored '57 Chevy station wagon for $150. The perfect vehicle for camping with the back seats folded down.

We traveled together for blissful months, sometimes staying for days in forests, settling only long enough in a log cabin in Idaho to save money. I wove multi-colored belts while Fred played gigs, gave astrology and tarot readings, and wrote. We planned to drive back to New York, sell the weavings, sell the car for money to fly to England, then spend a quiet winter in an Irish cottage owned by my mother, where Fred could write and I would make art.

In mid October we took off for the East Coast. Driving day and night, we took turns sleeping in the back, making the most of the powerful V-8 Chevy engine. Halfway across the country, mid-way between Idaho to New York, heavy rain fell on freeway rush hour traffic as Fred drove through Columbus, Ohio while I slept in the back. The Chevy hydroplaned, skidded sideways, bounced twice off an overpass, doing a complete 360 degree turn before limping to the side of the road. Amazingly we were unhurt, but only one forward gear survived on the Chevy, with no reverse, severe dents and scrapes, and a couple of broken windows. There would be no more freeway driving. We sold some woven belts to pay for immediate repairs, but in reality the Chevy was totaled, with no insurance. We had no choice but to drive at a snail's pace through the scenic countryside of Ohio and Pennsylvania exploring the smallest of back roads through Amish country— two simple, peaceful weeks of rural meandering from Columbus to Manhattan. Like the lightning speed Fred's fingers leapt up and down guitar frets, our life together had been speeding far too fast.

Before reaching New York, we drove through a landscape ablaze with fiery fall color, stopping to fill the back of the

Chevy with fallen leaves. In Manhattan we racked up dozens of parking tickets since we could only pull into spaces by driving forward where there was an easy exit with no backing up. At night we curled up under the leaves in the back of the station wagon. No one bothered us in the beat up old wreck of a car.

After several days of figuring out what to do, and selling more woven belts, we left Manhattan for Massachusetts where we abandoned the '57 Chevy in a Cambridge parking lot.

We never made it to Europe. And I have never been back to New York.

# 9. Running

On the sea front, deserted except for a bedraggled stray dog,
icy wind whips cold mist across my face.
With a hollow boom, waves pound the crumbling sea wall,
fling high white frothing spray,
suck back before the next assault.

I run, avoiding pebbles washed along the desolate promenade.
I run, not from anything, not to anything.
I run because I must.
I run on emotions that punch at me like the swell of the tide.
I run to light the fire of transformation,
to warm a cold and turbulent inner sea to steam,
to burn away the clinging scent of death.
I run to dredge up hidden emotions,
to raise them to the light
where spray and wind will wash them clean.
I run to keep myself alive in precious minutes of freedom
before returning to my mother's bed
where she lies in a semi-coma before her final breath.

Every morning, after I spoon-feed her breakfast
I drop my son at the nearby primary school,
hike the hill to the seafront,
climb over a low wall to the promenade,
stretch my legs against rusted railings
where the sea wall drops to a deserted beach below.

I gaze out along a line of tar-soaked breakwaters
disappearing below the waves,
yearly disintegrating under the weight of storm after storm,

keeping beaches from disappearing altogether
as water slams the southern coast.
High tide Channel spray coats my hair,
dampens my clothes, stings my eyes.


I turn left on the promenade and run
toward the Martello Tower.
I run hard and fast.
My chest hurts, my lungs cannot contain enough air
to thrust me forward out of sadness.
My throat rebels as I gasp for air.
Work, lungs, work!
Oxygen, burn this weight that pulls at me like a rusted anchor!
Raise this sorrow to the tipping point of letting go.
My chattering mind tells me I'm ready to let go,
but deep down, there is no escape
from the tie that binds a mother and child.
Roots are deeper than any unruly mind can fathom,
and won't let go.


I run as hard as I can
until the tightness of my chest screams STOP.
I arrive at the Martello tower,
a round concrete bastion of wartime ghosts,
built in 1810 to repel an invasion by Napoleon.
Memories rush in of an amusement arcade,
ice creams, frozen lollipops on carefree teenage summer days.
Days spent on steep pebble beaches,
thin towels spread to protect from
bumpy lumpy rudeness of the cold gray stones.
Now the arcade is closed forever.
The tower houses a museum, closed in winter.

Can the pain in my lungs lessen the suffering
my mother bears with such grim British stoicism?
The stiff upper lip.
Only once has she requested a pill to ease the pain.
I imagine it is too much pain for anyone to bear.
She denies her agony, but her contorted body tells me
otherwise.
Do I take on her suffering for her?
Isn't that what all children try to do for their mother?
"Be happy mom, mummy, or mother, please be well,"
must be the thought of every good child.

I endured her years of sadness,
her hidden undercurrents of bitter disappointment.
I ran from her sadness to Greece,
the land of Zorba, sunshine and dance.
I ran to America, land of movie magic and wide open space.
I ran to where emotions could be expressed,
laid out like colored saris on rocks
to dry and be bleached by the sun.
I ran to India to let go of any cord
that tied me to my mother's sorrow.

Now I run between scattered pebbles
thrown on the damp promenade.
I run past peeling-paint beach huts, padlocked for winter,
to where the sidewalk ends under Seaford Head.
From the last tarry stretch of shingled beach
I look toward towering chalk cliffs
stretching into the distance under the South Downs.
Chunks of concrete and tide-pools block my path,
the beach impassable at high tide.
I can go no further.

I turn back and run to face the endless
ordinariness and bursting intensity of waiting
for the inevitability and release of death for my mother.

# 10. The Tree Waterer

I am the tree waterer.

I sit beneath a giant redwood tree.
A peacock screams from the valley below.
No ordinary redwood this,
uprooted, trucked a thousand miles,
the last eighteen, up a rutted desert road.
They arrive, two trees per semi,
three times a week.

I am the tree waterer.

Forty-five minutes at each tree,
twelve hours a day
I sit, I move the hose.

Another peacock, an occasional cricket,
the sound of running water.
Silence.
I surrender.

I surrender to warm air, shadows,
juniper scent and sage.
I lose all track of time,
dissolve into bliss
in the garden of my Guru.

I move the hose,
my attention drawn to the traveling tree.
I pray water prayers for strong growth

held by the promise of the seed
so many years ago.

How many of us have been
uprooted, transplanted,
at one time or other in our life?
I chose to uproot from my land of birth,
a transplant to another country,
another way of wandering life.

My Guru, uprooted, transplanted
to a country far from birth,
perhaps his wish, but maybe not.
I do not think he chose this place to be.
He lives a choiceless way of life.

These trees? A Guru's whim?
Or the wish of one wanting to please
when she heard he missed
the lush green of his Indian life?

I do not question.
It is enough here on this hillside
by these massive noble trees
that I serve and tend with care
in this utopian experiment
to create an oasis in a desert

Trees, too, live a choiceless way of life.
Is their uprooting, transplanting by man
a violence against the way of trees?
Can they survive this uprooting?

A giant excavator gouged new homes,
smashed metal teeth into hardest rock
through a meager inch of earth.
Lifted from a semi by crane,
their unwrapped root-balls
transplanted into shallow bowls of solid stone

filled with backhoe loads of topsoil
composted to grow their sturdy roots.

I am the tree waterer.

I must believe my work is not in vain.
I must believe
as trees settle in their new land
tiny tendrils will reach beyond their roots
through compost rich dirt
to engage with walls of rock,
and with persistent pulse
crack wide the heavy stone,
break tiny pathways
to change the solid way of rock
to birth new soil,
inviting insect, microbe and mycelium.

I must believe the water
soaking down to thirsty roots
will feed green canopies in driest months,
invite cool water to this land
to create a lush and growing micro-clime.

Inside my head, a voice rings clear:
Do not believe

or cling to thoughts
or desires of what will be.

Everything will be taken from you in the end.

Receive this gift of being
on this hillside

with this flow of water
to feed this tree.

In this moment, it is enough.

# 11. The Raspberry Farm

I HAD a farm in Oregon for three years—two acres, close to Mt Hood. It would be a stretch, though, to call it a farm since the cultivated area was little more than three quarters of an acre, planted with old raspberry bushes. The bushes had produced berries for almost twenty-five years, with the weariest vines starting to thin along the neat lines of rows, though most still grew robust and strong, producing plentiful fruit. The berries grew organically in the ideal berry-growing conditions of northwest Oregon.

At the time, I lived in an apartment in Seattle with my boyfriend, a banjo player/vocalist with a bluegrass band, Appalachian Downshift, who worked alongside me selling for my small crafts business. The band's lead guitarist lived in a small town close to Mt. Hood, and the fiddle player lived in Eugene. After an excellent year of sales from my business, with money to spare, and the desire to spend more time outside a city, it made sense to invest in a small piece of land where both of us would benefit. He'd have a place to stay if he'd lined up a weekend gig in Oregon, and could also sell at Portland Saturday Market, a market I'd sold at previously when I'd lived in Portland. And whenever my commitments in the Puget Sound allowed, I would drive down to the farm for much needed days of peace and quiet.

The place was ideal; a two acre parcel with a two bedroom single wide mobile home at a reasonable price, sold by the owner, a widow with ten acres surrounding mine on two sides. We shared a well. Most of her property was covered by second growth timber, with the rest cultivated in raspberries.

My partner went to work with a weed-eater, keeping fast-growing vegetation in check between the raspberry rows, leaving more than enough greenery for hungry insects to munch before they discovered the tender young raspberry shoots. In spring, I spent blissful days alone at the farm caring for the bushes, cutting back dead canes that had fruited the previous summer, pruning and tying new vines to wires stretched from post to post across the field. Hour after happy hour I worked at my own pace up and down the rows, hidden from the world, with the occasional bird and birdsong for company. City stress fell away.

Behind the raspberry field we set up a tipi to live closer to the ground when weather permitted, away from the metal box of the mobile home, and also as an extra space for visiting guests to stay.

By the end of June the vines started to bear fruit. A lot of fruit. What would we do with all those berries! We were approached by a man with a berry picking machine—a monster piece of equipment that could straddle bushes as it rumbled up and down rows and shake berries from their canes. Neighbors recommended we hire local or itinerant pickers. Neither option appealed to us; we weren't there often enough to supervise the harvest, or to organize selling the crop.

"How about we give the berries away," I suggested.

"Good idea, how we going to do that?"

"Throw a party. Have a celebration. You and your band can play and we'll invite people to come and pick as many berries as they want."

And so a yearly tradition (although a very short one) of the "Raspberry Rendezvous" began. The event took place the third Saturday in July, the weekend after the Oregon Country Fair where Appalachian Downshift had a gig and I sold my hand-painted clothing. We printed posters and invited a wide circle of friends and acquaintances, welcome to visit any time in the afternoon and long evening for a potluck, music, and free-for-all berry picking, bringing their own buckets and baskets to fill with as many raspberries as they could carry. Visitors were welcome to stay overnight in the tipi or set up their own tents.

Imagine the joyful laughter of berry-stained children running up and down the rows stopping only to gorge on handfuls of the perfectly ripe fruit. If they were corralled long enough to assist an adult with harvesting berries to take home, it was a one-in-the-mouth, one-in-the-bucket kind of berry picking. There were more than enough berries for everyone, plus future feasts for passing birds.

Imagine, too, the banquet that guests brought for the potluck: salads, casseroles, pies, fresh baked bread, homemade yogurt, fresh juices and free-flowing wine. As the sun cast longer and longer shadows, music echoed through the raspberry rows. Appalachian Downshift and friends in another band alternated sets well into the night with additional musicians joining in to jam. Merry berry pickers danced till the early morning hours.

The first year of the event, word got around local bars about a party with live music out in a raspberry field where anyone was welcome. Maybe the word got out because my banjo playing friend had visited a bar earlier in the day. Bikers and pickups full of rowdy locals arrived, beer and wine in hand, more interested in drinking and partying than anything to do with raspberries, except when they peed between the rows. After a drunken fight, some of the men left. Later we found one man passed out snoring in the raspberry bushes; we didn't disturb him.

In the morning, we served a raspberry pancake breakfast topped with, of course, raspberry syrup. Many guests later brought us gifts of jam or syrup, or wine they had made from our berries. And we had a freezer full of raspberries.

After events of the first year, and the fact that my banjo friend had quit drinking, we requested visitors not to bring alcohol the second year, and the local bar crowd wasn't invited. The event was far mellower, with Appalachian Downshift playing, plus hypnotic dance tunes of a marimba band. It was also the last year of the "Raspberry Rendezvous".

With my relationship with banjo man disintegrating, I rented out the mobile home to friends. At that time too, I frequently traveled overseas. After returning from a trip to India, and excited to stay out on the land for a few days to acclimatize, I drove right past the property, not recognizing the place. I had failed to see the familiar landmark of my neighbor's tall trees, and missed the farm entirely. I realized her land had been clear-cut. I was heartbroken.

I doubled back and stopped at my neighbor's house. She tearfully told me that the man she'd been married to for two years divorced her as soon as he finished helping renovate her house. He sued for a large divorce settlement. As her only option to avoid losing her home, she cut and sold the valuable second growth timber. She was a vulnerable widow, the victim of an unscrupulous con man.

Within a year, the water table dropped and I wondered if the clear-cutting had anything to do with the shared well going dry. I was given the option to either drill a new well on my land, or pay half the cost for my neighbor's well to be dug much deeper, although it was already deep. On top of that, the farm was no longer a quiet sanctuary after the arrival of noisy kennels on land adjacent to the property.

I chose to sell the farm for about the same price I paid, quit my business in Seattle and moved to Santa Fe.

# 12. The Flying Mattress

Yes! He arrives this afternoon.
Two months since I saw him last.
Tonight he'll stay at my desert home
before tomorrow's errands in Santa Fe.
My wild, sexy, Scottish artist friend,
handsome, larger-than-life, man of the untamed hills.
In half an hour he'll be here.
Did I say sexy, yes, sexy
as in sensual jungle-animal sexy.
And I haven't had sex in months.

And now here in my living room,
his resonant voice tingles through my bones,
his chuckle and hypnotic eyes slide deep
into my veins like quicksilver.
He, of the wild long hair.
Part Merlin bard, part artist, part Pan (about three quarters),
dripping with soul, and song,
laughter, and unspoken sadness.
I am more than ready to melt
in his aura and dissolve in his wiry arms.

But no. We must remain friends.
How could I face his girlfriend up north
who waits in sagebrush hill country,
in the home they built of stained glass,
adobe and scrounged wood,
a home touched with the magic of mushroom trips,
medicine wheels and over-abundant gardens?
We must remain friends, nothing more,

though everyone knows both he and his girlfriend
are free and easy with their loving.

We drive half an hour to town.
Dinner at a Mexican café.
My boundaries melt like ice cream in a heat wave,
my brain, jello.
His voice seduces with ripe magnolias and peonies,
one shot of tequila and I'll sacrifice everything
for a night of melt and mingle, liquid bones,
flashes, sparks and soft skin sweeps.

And now I can't eat. I can't hear what he's saying.
I am almost completely lost.
Forget the hot tamales in hot jalapeno tomatillo sauce.
This man is hot. I'm hot.
But somewhere still, there's that NO that won't let go,
the stern NO that niggles and squiggles inside my head,
the voice of mother, father,
schoolteacher, preacher, judge and jury.
What should I do? What will I do?

Now we're outside in the cool,
strolling the fragrant Plaza night air
alive with Indian spirits and old adobe.
Tourists float by in a blur of Indian blanket jackets
expensive turquoise trinkets and cowboy boots.
He's handing me a joint.
I'm smoking it and I'm out-of-it flying.
So long since I smoked.

And now the world is suddenly dreamy,
everything-perfect wordless,
there's no immediate decision to make.
Nano-second to nano-second.
The moon is huge,
I'm out there shining with the moon as it floods the town.
I'm lightning flashing in the Sangre de Christos,
the smell of sage brush flooding the high desert air.

Evening light weaves sharp and clear,
and soft and misty.
Especially sharp and clear,
tension jumping between me and the electric being by my side.
My brain drifts the cosmos,
my body, taut wires holding a boat in a storm.
His too. I know it. He knows it.
We don't say a word. We can't talk about it.
We're too much in, or out, of our heads.
How to come back down to the land of sex and earth?

Will we take it to the mattress tonight?

We walk in electric silence, tension mounting,
scarcely able to bear the slightest touch of skin.
Each step and his jeans
sound the sensual shuffle of a snare drum,
each footfall the pulse of a slow drumbeat.

Now the chill of the mountain night creeps in.
Am I quivering, or shivering?

In no shape to drive, but with alcohol level
closer to legal than his, I take the wheel.

My brain anywhere but concentrating on the freeway.
Synapses wrestle unruly creatures of conscience.
To fuck or not to fuck.


And now we're flying down the highway under the full moon.
On either side, the desert: white, cool, silent.
Splinters of ghost light etch the horizon.
Only the occasional late night trucker roars east to Texas.
A speeding road hog flashes past.
A pickup piled high with furniture pulls in front.


One moment I'm floating in dreamtime,
hypnotized by white lines on the road,
then, tension prickles like a shoplifter
before she sneaks her prize.
Neither of us speaks.
What am I going to do?
We've been good friends for so long.
Pleasures of one night would change everything.
Do we want to go there?
Do I want to go there? Does he want to go there?
My brain tosses between the danger of pleasurable possibilities
and the safety of 'no need for immediate action'.
After all, I *am* just driving down a road.


What's that! O My God! In the air ahead!
Flying straight at the car.
A huge kite? A giant slab of cheese sailing in the moonlight.
A piece broken off the moon?
No, it's blowing from the furniture pickup in front.


Smack. It hits the freeway.
I can't avoid it. I'm driving too fast.
If I swerve I'll hit it. I'll hit it if I don't.

There's no time. My eyes are saucers.
I grip the steering wheel.
Drive on! Straight ahead.
Brake. Don't brake.
Get the wheels in line to pass over the top of it.
Go. Keep going.
Before I have time to breathe, the mattress
(thank God, a single mattress)
passes right between the wheels of the car.
I pull over to the side of the road, we look at each other.
We explode with laughter.

I never did have sex with my artist friend.

# 13. The Geode

WHILE sorting through and selectively clearing accumulated clutter from a drawer a few years back, I came across a small geode stashed inside a jeweled rawhide box. I wondered how many years it had been since I exiled the geode to hide among the jumble of forgotten treasures at the back of the bottom drawer. I couldn't remember. Perhaps I'd banished it during one of my living-space Zen sweeps, or perhaps I'd thrown it in the drawer while unpacking after one of many moves.

The long-neglected object of beauty first caught my eye many years before on a pilgrimage to sacred Hindu and Buddhist temples sculpted into a rugged mountainside in Maharasthra, India. On the dusty earth outside the temples, merchants had set up tables where they sold crystals, polished rocks and gems mined from the surrounding hills. As soon as I saw the geode, a split rock the size of a small pheasant's egg, the geode seduced me with its exquisite beauty, two miniature caves lined with sparkling crystal geometries. It was far more ancient and thrilling than any of the centuries old, laboriously carved temples. The rock existed long before Gods and Goddesses were worshipped by humans. It spoke to me of the beauty of Mother Earth and hinted at ancient mysteries older than any measurable human time.

I held the split rock in the palm of my left hand, feeling its subtle vibrations. From deep within I heard it whisper silently to me: "Take me home with you; I belong in your life. I will teach you the secret of my inner treasure."

I handed over a fistful of rupees.

I left India, and for years the precious geode journeyed with me, the two halves of the open stone sparkling on altars and shelves wherever I lived. I often marveled at its magical crystal symmetry flashing in rays of sunlight. Such beauty!

I thought I understood the power and potency of crystals. But even though the rock glittered and shone so brightly for me, it never quite seemed to fulfill the promise of teaching me the secret of its inner treasure. What was I missing? Was its inner treasure only the hypnotic beauty of the crystals I gazed at from time to time? Was it only another pretty rock? Was I crazy to have thought a rock could speak to me? I pushed the geode further and further from sight as other objects of delight caught my eye, until one day I put the rock in the rawhide box and tossed it unceremoniously into the shadows.

The day I rediscovered the rock, I returned it to its rightful place of honor in the daylight, on my altar. But there was a difference. I closed the two halves of the stone to seal it back to its original egg-like form. I honored the secret of its inner treasure—as I had realized my own.

SEVERAL years after the acquisition of the geode, I took part in a training with a Peruvian shaman, high in the Incan Andes, where the power of Pachamama, Mother Goddess Earth, flows through all of life. Before one of a series of seven initiations, one for each of the chakras, I prepared to disappear through a hole in the ground into a dark tunnel, with no flashlight or headlamp, and no idea of the height and width of the passage, or the length of my underground journey before I would reenter daylight. I thought I would be afraid. I remembered as a child being terrified when sent to fetch an item from the depths of a shadowy for basement.

But for some reason I didn't feel scared. I wasn't afraid. I bowed my forehead to the earth, said a short prayer to Pachamama and lowered myself into the ground feeling like a mole—those amazing blind creatures weighing only four or five ounces, who burrow up to fifteen feet an hour and who, in a minute, can race through eighty feet of tunnel—but speed was not the objective. My pulse slowed as the earth welcomed me; raw damp air filled my lungs; earthen smells entered my nostrils. I ran my hands over the smooth surface of cold walls that pressed against my body, walls that embraced me with birth-canal darkness as I inched forward, half crawling, half squirming, feeling my way deeper and deeper along the narrow tunnel until I felt it open into a small inky-black cavern. I paused, motionless in my underground world, everything silent except for the steady rhythm of my pulse as I relaxed and melted into the space.

Almost immediately a wave of light flooded the blackness. But the explosion of light was not from any outside source. It burst from inside *me*. Radiance, brighter and more golden than sunlit honey, flooded every cell of my tissue, bone and being. Everywhere, a flood of luminescent, incandescent light. In that moment I knew the healing force of light that lives within the dark womb of the world, within every one of us and within every hollow space of the universe. I was filled with the immeasurable power of the earth, the power of the womb and the power of Pachamama.

THE day I rediscovered the geode in my drawer, I closed the two halves of the rock in my hand and remembered that moment when the luminous potential at the hollow center within the dark void had spoken to me, and knew the flame of healing dream-light energy flares brightest in the pitchy black.

Give me the quiet resting place of a moonless night. Give me the darkness of the womb from which all life ignites. Today

I am no longer enamored or dazzled by the glitz and glamour of the geode's crystal revelry or silken smoothness of the outer shell, but know the hidden world of light that cannot be seen by human eye. Possibilities pour from the space within, and it is the depths and flavor of inner connection that excite me as I run my fingers over the sealed rock. The stone has taught me well. And now, whenever I need to be reminded of the limitless inner world, I curl up in the secret darkness of the geode womb and journey in a land of infinite light.

# 14. War

When you think of someone sleeping,
you probably picture them lying still and passive as death,
except for the gentle rise and fall of breath.
Perhaps you imagine them dreaming sweet dreams,
wandering through a land of mystery and magic.

You obviously haven't seen or heard my man sleep.
I have. I share his action-packed bed.
Many nights, around 3 am,
especially if he's gorged on a midnight snack,
he begins to whimper.
He jerks, shakes, mutters
unintelligible words in a high-pitched whine.
His eyelids flutter.

His legs twitch like a sleeping dog
who dreams of chasing rabbits.
His chest heaves. He pants.
A forearm reaches up to ward off an imaginary enemy.
Then, with a grunt of effort, he pushes both arms
hard against the blankets as if they were chains,
or a mesh of tangled wire from which he must escape.
Intensity of his nightmare builds,
volume of his muttering escalates.
I retreat to the farthest edge of the bed.

His movements grow wild.
He shouts and growls.
His taut back pushes rigid against the mattress,
while slack-skinned arms and legs flail

like an octopus harpooned to the ocean floor.
He kicks away the sheets.
He twists in terror. He punches the air.
He yells, "I'm going to kill you, mother fucker!"

His drained limbs go limp.
He sinks back into the bed.
Sleeping, he sobs without tears.
I reach over to put my arms around him
to comfort his troubled sleep.
He shoves me away, unable to tell if I am friend
or foe in his hidden world of terror.
Still sleeping, he rolls away slowly, gathers speed,
clutching the bedclothes, dragging the blanket after him.
He rolls, he tips over the edge of the bed
into the shelter of a jungle ditch.
He hits the floor and wakes, bewildered.

I imagine what he is thinking:
"Honey, they'll never draft my grandkids
into the army, will they?"

# 15. Voice of The Heart

I KNOW I have a problem when the dirt road tapers narrower and narrower, the minivan fishtails uneasily through increasingly squishy grit and drifting sand, and I see nothing familiar in the desert landscape of sage and occasional hardy juniper. I ask myself: how did I end up driving on the wrong road? Later, I ask the question: WHY did I end up on the wrong road?

The 'how' question is easier to answer than the 'why.' After leaving the parking area near the group campsite, I set out to drive the seven or eight miles to a highway bordering Grand Staircase-Escalante National Monument. Then, without thinking, at a fork in the road, I took a wrong turn to the right. Two miles later the road abruptly ended. Irritated by my mistake, I swung the vehicle around and hurried back to the main dirt road. That was where I made my second mistake. Again, without thinking, I turned left at the fork instead of right and headed back the way I'd come. I drove past the parking area without seeing it and disappeared even further into the desert.

Now, after not driving for more than a week, after the rush and chaos of goodbyes to friends with whom I've been camping, plus the hazy light of a blowing desert sand storm, my usually sharp perceptions and sense of direction are dangerously unreliable. How incredibly foolish I feel at my lack of awareness.

I know I must turn back before the road peters out completely, although I am sure the road must lead somewhere. This is, after all, a National Monument. Wouldn't there be signs saying a road is a dead end? But then, with nearly a thousand miles of public access roads spread over 1.7 million acres, perhaps not all the roads are well marked—something I have already learned.

On what is now no more than a sandy track, there are no turnouts where I can safely turn around; driving further doesn't seem like a good idea either. I stop the van and take several deep breaths. My only option is to make the one-hundred-and-eighty degree turn with extreme caution, however many back-and-forth maneuvers it might take: a few inches forward with wheels to the right, back up six inches to the left. Repeat. Repeat again. But I am not cautious enough. I am helpless, with a sinking feeling in my gut, while in slow motion I feel the front wheels sinking into the sand. Although the shoulder of the road appears solid, the deceptive reddish-pink crust has quietly given way, trapping its prey with a powdery grip.

Now I'm stuck. What should I do next? I think of times I've been stuck in snow or ice. I try rocking the van to and fro with gentle, then sudden bursts of acceleration. But that exercise proves futile, only spinning the wheels, and with each back and forth the vehicle burrows deeper into the soft sand like a stinkbug scurrying to hide from the light.

I climb out of the van to assess the situation. I know there's no way I can free the van without help. My cell phone battery is dead; even if it wasn't, there is no reception out here in the wilderness. And even if I could call AAA it would be useless since they won't tow from remote dirt roads. I look around in all directions, but all I see is scrubby desert through a haze of blowing sand, with a line of pretty rust-red hills visible on the horizon. At least I have a nice view, although appreciation of the fine view lasts barely a minute.

Sudden panic rushes through me. With a surge of anger, I punch my fists at the sky. Surprised at my ferocity, I shriek F U C K! I grab my orange emergency whistle out of my pack and rip the air with three long blasts even though I know no one will hear. How stupid I am. How fucking stupid.

Once the fire of my outburst cools, I examine my possibilities. I have no shovel. Only a plastic meal bowl and a spoon. I position myself with my back to the blowing, stinging grit, and slowly and methodically scoop sand away from the sunken tires, then drag floor mats from the front of the van and position them strategically behind the wheels. But when I try rocking the van backwards and forwards again, the spinning tires grab the floor mats, pull them under and fling them aside. When I try putting my camping tarp under the wheels, the slippery blue plastic immediately shreds. It's useless. Close to tears, I wipe away sweat and sand from my face, neck, and inside my clothes where sand has trickled in and mixed with sweat, blending together to the texture of sandpaper. I'd much rather be enjoying a salt scrub at my local spa. I give up.

It is a Friday, about 5:30pm, mid-May. The van, like a beached whale, straddles the narrow track on a diagonal, the front end held fast in the sand, leaving no room for cars to pass. Anyone driving up must stop. Surely, on an early summer evening before a weekend, campers, hikers and tourists will flock to visit the National Monument. Surely, at least some of them will venture down this back road on their way to an obscure campsite that only they know. And surely, some hardy soul will be traveling in a hefty SUV or pickup, preferably with a powerful winch attached, to easily free a woman and minivan held hostage by the desert wind and sand. There are still several daylight hours left for that knight in four-wheel-drive to rescue this damsel in distress.

Trusting someone will arrive before nightfall, I decide not to leave and hike for help this evening. Hot sand blows horizontal across the desert, showing no sign of letting up. Staying inside my vehicle, even in the heat, seems the best option to await my rescuer.

In the shelter of my van, an old gold Previa named 'The Golden Bubble', things don't look so bad. I have a can of smoked oysters, a couple of meal bars, and a small bag of raisins I've saved for my drive back to the Pacific Northwest. My water bottle is three-quarters full. I have my sleeping bag and a sleeping pad that feels as luxurious as sleeping on a cloud of down. I have a novel that, at almost one-thousand-five-hundred pages, weighs two-and-a-half pounds. I brought the book along on my trip to southern Utah for rest area moments of escapist reading away from disciplined wide-eyed highway driving. Except for the persistent whistle of blowing wind, sand spitting at the side of the van, and the temperature several degrees warmer than comfortable, what more could I want for passing a quiet, peaceful evening in a nationally protected wildlife area.

The evening drags on with no sign of an approaching vehicle, and when I step out of the van to scan the horizon there's no hint of a distant dust trail rising above a road in any direction. There's no sound except constantly blowing fine grit hitting the van. The sun slowly eases toward the horizon. At least, if I must walk out for help, I know which direction is west, although after today's miscalculations I'm afraid I might still end up heading down the wrong road; the thought of snakes, too, does little to give me confidence.

I eat the smoked oysters and settle in for the remaining hours of daylight to read my book, "A Suitable Boy" by Vikram Seth. My mind distracted, I struggle through several paragraphs, then, disgusted by the description of a tannery scene, I toss the book aside. I laugh at the absurdity of my predicament. Here I am, stuck and lost in the Utah desert, reading a graphic stomach-churning scene of an Indian tannery part-way through a huge Austen-like tome of manners. I'd rather lie back and listen to the rising, falling chorus of the wind.

Now I consider the question: Why have I been placed in desert detention? In two days time I am expected at my ex-husband's seventieth birthday party in the Bay Area. Then a couple of days later I am due to stay with a friend in Oregon. Now, there's no way I'll make either date unless I'm rescued in the next two hours, which seems less and less likely as the sun slides closer to the glowing edge of the world. I should be half-way across Nevada by now. Perhaps I am not meant to visit either my ex-husband or my friend. But I doubt that that is why I am being held overtime in the desert.

I think back to the previous year when I had wondered how to celebrate a significant upcoming birthday in a meaningful way. I had wanted to do something special, something to set the stage for what I considered the beginning of my 'third act.' I settled on participating in a yearlong 'Soulcraft Immersion' underworld journey with a group of thirteen participants and two guides who would meet four times during the year in wilderness settings. In between the wilderness meetings we would participate in a 'cyber talking stick' online. The third gathering would include a vision quest.

I have now completed the third gathering, spending eight days in the desert. For four days I fasted on only water, and for three of those days endured a solo vision quest in an isolated area in a ten-foot diameter circle with only a sleeping bag and a notebook. Proud to have completed the vision quest ordeal, happy to have accomplished the most challenging part of the yearlong commitment, now here I am, stuck in the sand. Did I miss something? What part of the vision quest didn't I get? Obviously the desert isn't finished with me yet. At least now I have considerably more shelter than in my limited vision space where I was subjected to intense heat, cold, stinging sand-laden wind, plus a brief rain/lightning storm. And now I have food. But, here, there is no buddy system routine of pebble placement for accidents or emergencies, and no group waiting to welcome me back into community. Out here, no one knows where I am. The group and guides think I'm driving on a freeway back to civilization. My ex-husband might miss me when I don't show up for his birthday, my friend in Eugene might wonder why I don't visit, but neither would be particularly worried. Family in Washington State doesn't expect me back for almost a week. I am utterly alone. What if I walk out in the wrong direction, don't meet any people, collapse in the heat, get bit by a rattlesnake, black widow, tarantula…? Movie images stream through my mind of emaciated men staggering through the desert crying out for water. I still don't have an answer to why I'm stranded in this wasteland, even if it is a National Monument.

Before settling in for the star-filled night, I stuff my backpack with essentials in case my hike out takes longer than it should. For a while I lie awake watching shooting stars streak across the sky above the sunroof of the van, then sleep surprisingly well. After the previous week of sleeping on the ground, the safety of the van feels secure and womblike.

First light creeps from behind the eastern hills. I scribble a note and stick it to the inside of the windshield with a band-aid: "Gone for help. Back soon." What else could I write?

I pull on my pack and hike back along the road in the cool air before dawn, happy knowing the sun will be behind me when it rises. The wind too is behind me, the sandstorm still blowing, tossing flurries of dirt against my pack, but at least I'm not walking head-on into the stinging grit. I head north until the track bends west. At first I worry how far I must walk before knowing I'm headed in the right direction, but then, after about a mile, I recognize the parking lot turn-off on my left. But why are there no campers, no cars on the roads? It's the weekend. Perhaps something has happened to the world out there, and I'm the last to know.

I hike briskly before the sun is high, but soon tire, my body still drained from the four-day fast. I walk slower and slower. Age takes its toll, even though I think I'm fitter than most at my age. Resting from rapidly increasing heat in the minimal shade of a rock pile by the road, I realize how depleted and tired I am. After finishing my last meal bar I take small sips of water and allow myself to be mesmerized by the dusty-red, orange, pink, and copper hues of the distant hills. Their subtle beauty dissolves my fears, my concerns about the van, and the knowledge of how little water I have left with several miles still to hike. I don't want to get up. Perhaps I can rest until a car drives up. I close my eyes and surrender to the moment.

Suddenly a clear voice echoes inside my head: "You have a brave heart."

I know that voice! Now my second question is answered. I know WHY I am stuck in the desert.

Toward the end of my vision quest, along with many eventful dreams and moments of realization, I received a vision of an Indian warrior who shared a short clear message beginning with the words: "You have a brave heart," followed by a sentence about helping indigenous people. I wrote down his words, which seemed significant at the time, if somewhat trite. After our individual vision quests ended, the group met to share each person's experience. When it was my turn to speak, I talked with gratitude about the highs, lows, ecstatic moments, physical and mental hardships, dreams and numinous insights I had experienced. But when I came to share my vision of the Indian warrior, I told them how clichéd it felt for an Indian warrior to show up on a vision quest, as if straight from the set of a B-grade made-for-TV new-age movie.

Now I see my arrogance. You do not dismiss even the smallest of gifts from a Vision Quest, however clichéd they might seem. Now I am grateful to hear the echo of those words. They give me the strength to get up, pick up my pack and keep walking down the desert road. I am no longer afraid, only tired and hot as the sun climbs higher and higher in the sky. I walk for miles, welcoming the voice that resonates in my heart, repeating over and over again the words: "You have a brave heart."

Two hundred yards from the highway, a small car is parked by the road. Next to it, a man and a woman are packing up a tent. Exhausted and thirsty, with tears of relief now staining my cheeks, I tell the couple about my vehicle stuck in the sand.

"Oh, my," the woman says as she hands me a bottle of water, "we'd better find you a tow truck."

"We watched you walking up the road," says the man. "We commented how inspiring it was to see a courageous woman choosing to hike and camp alone in the desert!"

The couple gives me a ride to the ranger station in Escalante. After a short wait, a tow truck driver picks me up and drives me back across the desert to the stranded van. Within ten minutes the vehicle is pulled free from the sand, I sign over a large sum of money on my credit card and drive with caution back along the narrow road, following the tow truck out of the park.

But wait, that is not the end of the story.

IT is too late for me to make it to my ex's birthday party, and besides, I long to be home as soon as possible. I decide to drive straight through to the Northwest with only short stops at rest areas to sleep. The miles fly by. I relish the freedom of highway racing after my ordeal in the sucking sand.

On Sunday morning, approaching a rest area near the Idaho/Oregon border, I glance in my rear view mirror and see a highway patrol car following close behind. There are no flashing lights, but I still instinctively wonder what I might have done wrong, besides driving too fast and for too many hours the night before. The patrol car follows me off the highway at the exit and then pulls up next to my van in the parking lot.

Then I understand the reason the officer has stopped at this rest area, and it's not for me. Next to the restrooms, a small group of people have gathered around an elderly man sitting on a low stool. In front of him on the grass is a blanket on which he has laid out a display of small handmade carvings. Not knowing why, I feel intuitively drawn to reach the old man before the officer. I walk quickly toward the vendor, the patrolman marching close behind.

Then I see it. On the blanket, surrounded by eagles, wolves, bears and other small creatures carved from cottonwood, lies the exquisitely carved figure of the Indian warrior who had spoken to me during my vision quest and on my hike!

The officer now stands stiff and authoritarian by the vendor, leaning in, ready to speak, undoubtedly to tell him to move on, but before he can say a word, I snatch up the carved figure and launch into the story of how this is the same warrior who appeared to me on my recent vision quest, and how this warrior gave me courage while I walked out of the desert the previous day after becoming lost with my van trapped in the sand. The small group listens to my tale, enthralled. I watch a hint of tears well-up in the eyes of the elderly woodcarver who looks like he might be Indian himself, but mostly I notice the reaction of the patrolman.

The officer's whole demeanor has shifted. While at first, he had been puffed up to a fully aggressive, 'I'm-about-to-exert-my-authority-and-send-you-packing' stance with hands hovering by his gun belt, now he has softened. I detect a hint of a smile across his previously stern expression as he squats, and without a word, picks up and examines several of the small carvings. "I'll take this one," he says as he pulls out his wallet. "My son will like this wolf." He pays, thanks the vendor, nods to me and leaves.

"You showed up exactly the right time," says the woodcarver. "Someone complained about me selling here, so I'd been expecting a visit from the cops. Thank you, miss."

I buy the small carving of the Indian warrior. "Thank you, I will cherish this and all it means to me."

The old man looks at me fully in the eye and I hear, in an internal voice that sounds remarkably like the one I had previously heard: "You have a brave heart."

# 16. Rivers

Short chronological scenes of rivers on 6 continents (Europe, Africa, N. America, Asia, S. America, and Australia).


## 1. STEPPING STONES

Hounsden gutter, North London, Europe.

Chubby fingers dabble icy water.
Smooth pebbles tumble through my tiny hands.
Water ripples, burbles, gurgles,
swills along the shallow riverbed.

"Common on" he urges,
wading, splashing to the other bank.
"'s too deep."
"Not too deep."
"Me stay and play."
Springtime water swirls fast above my brother's knees.
"Baby, baby's afraid of water."
"Am not."

But I am. I want to cross, but how?
Rocks lurk slick below the surface.
I AM afraid.

"Baby, baby, baby," he taunts.
"Won't even hold my hand to cross."
Tears leak down cold cheeks.
I give up.

Two boy scouts wander the footpath to the creek.
"Hey little girl. Why are you crying?"
"Want to cross but I'm scared."
"We'll fix that," says the taller boy,
swooping down, lifting me,
striding across slippery stepping stones
gently placing me on the other side.

☼

## 2. KADUNA MEANS CROCODILE

Kaduna River, Northern Nigeria, Africa.

The muddy river, a torrent swollen
from monsoon rain races flood stage fast.
Leafy branches bend,
sway, dip, through the swift current.
High water challenges riverbank trees.

Africans glide like river otters
across the Kaduna river flood,
bellies resting on hollow calabashes,
oar-hands paddling swift and rhythmic
through the brown-green flood.
Inside the calabashes, market goods,
banana, cassava, mangos, yams,
cloth for villages across the river.

How can these men survive this swirling flood,
this watery home to crocodiles?

After thousands of years of sharing crocodile waters,
for these fearless Kaduna men,
an ordinary event.

## 3. FOG

River Ouse, Sussex, England, Europe.

Partying in a south coast town,
all sense of time is lost.
Will I reach Newhaven Bridge
before the midnight closing?

Dense fog shrouds the coastal road.
With cautious driving through the swirling mist,
I am too late.
Five minutes past midnight, and the bridge has closed.

Along the inland detour,
ghost trees hover like hungry vultures
beside the River Ouse.

Easing slowly through the drifting gloom
I cross the old Southease bridge.
Perhaps it was in dense fog like this
Virginia Woolf filled her pockets with rocks,
waded into this river and out of time,
her lifeless body drifting underwater,
to a downstream bank nearby.

## 4. HIGH WATER

East Fork of the Big Wood River, Idaho, North America.

High in the Sawtooth mountains.
High with friends,

high-roller friends, heirs to fortunes.
Shy, recently from England,
I have never known friends like this before

Driving, lurching up the rocky track
beside the East Fork Big Wood river,
we are laughing, high.
At a river ford,the driver does not hesitate,
though the river runs fast and snow-melt high,
though the vehicle is a spotless new Mercedes.

The car high ends on rocks
half-way through the flooding river.
Water rushes above the level of the floor.
The driver pushes open his door.
The passenger pushes open his door.
Water gushes in and races through.

I have never known such a high-end car before.
A river runs through it
and they laugh. They roar with laughter.

How can they do that?
I have never seen such privileged
disregard for wealth before.

## 5. FALL IDYLL

Big Wood River, Idaho, North America.

At a bend in the Big Wood River
low-water meanders beneath wind-rustled aspens,
the surface a quivering reflection of golden leaves.
Oblique light glances through rippled echoes
of slow swirled eddies,
painting shadows on smooth rocks below.

My child, asleep on my back,
perhaps dreams water dreams.

Dappled rainbows dart from shallows to depths and back.
Tuned to the gurgle and trickle of the stream,
mesmerized by ever-shifting currents
I cast, and cast again, for a fresh trout dinner.

I pause, motionless, to fill memory banks
with sunlit water gliding over submerged leaves,
contentment in a change of season,
and river sounds
of a golden afternoon
by a mountain stream in fall.

## 6. VOLCANO

Columbia River, Sauvies Island, Oregon, North America.

On Sauvies Island,
by the Columbia River north of Portland,
we bask on a nude beach
on a summer day.
Across the water, Mt. St Helens,
made famous since two months,
when explosive power
blasted the mountain wide,
ash blackened the eastern sky,
mud flows swallowed forests,
and rivers changed their course forever.

On this lazy afternoon
the mountain rests, peaceful.
Contented on my sun-warm towel
after cold Columbia swimming
I gaze as tiny puffs of cloud drift by.

Then little puffs of smoke, not clouds, plume,
then billow from the sleeping crater.
The mountain has more to say.

Are we far enough away?
What if the wind shifts west
to smother the land with ash?
After the big blow,
cars sputtered, refused to start.
Stranded people gasped,
choked on the thick gray dust.

Fast clothed,
we huddle at a transistor radio.
What way does the wind blow?
Is this another historic event?
It is time to leave this Columbia River beach.

## 7. ON AN INDIAN RIVER

Poona River, Maharasthra, India, Asia.

For my son's birthday,
a boat ride on the olive-green Poona river,
lazy gliding downstream past mud-red shores.

On smooth shoreline rocks
washer women pound clothes,
stretch bright saris to sunshine dry.
Before the monsoon
low water faded vegetation
colonizes the silted river bank.

We float past burning ghats, past crowded bridges
where horn-beeping rickshaws,
cyclists, men-drawn carts, holy cows
work their daily routine.

We eat birthday cake,
we drift,
and sing a celebration song.

# 8. CURRENT

John Day River, Oregon, North America.


Current runs
fast, high
from late spring rains.


Buoyed safely
on an inner tube
I push away from the bank.


Like a wild animal in raucous play,
Current swirls, tilts,
rushes, pushes, pummels.


And like an animal at play,
Current won't give up,
plays rough and rowdy
to engage its strange pink playmate.


The tube upends,
tosses me into the flood,
Current drags me under.
I gasp, I struggle for air.


Current races too fast
for panicked swimming.
My heart races.


I tumble with the river
turn on my back and drift feet first,

floating, yielding to Current.
No more fight. I give up.
Current wins its playful game.

And in surrender,
Current floats me safely back to shore.

## 9. HOT SPRINGS

Rio Grande, New Mexico, North America.

We hike
the steep, narrow, rocky canyon path
down,
down,
to steaming hot springs pools
south of Taos by the Rio Grande.
Blissful soaking.
Just that.

## 10. RIVER RAFTING

Urubamba River, Peru, South America.

After a night of journeying
with shamans,
sleepless by the Inca trail,
for the day ahead,
a gentle float,

high in the Andes
on the Urubamba River

Two rafts.
In my raft, those who held ceremony
still half-way in other dreaming worlds,
vulnerable to this one,
hoping to navigate the river with flow and ease.

In the other raft,
Brazilians who chose not to journey,
who shriek and taunt and shout,
who hurl buckets of icy water
onto our shuddering little raft
between splashing, soaking, heaving waves
sluicing down steep rapids of the raging river.

After traveling through dreaming realms,
not a gentle float but
a hard, cold price to re-enter
the human world.

## 11. HAVASUPAI

Colorado River, Grand Canyon, Arizona, North America.

Below Havasupai native village,
I hike alone to join friends at the falls,
looking for cliff-face metal rungs,
the ladder down,
to the river's edge,

to a silvery plunge of falls
in the Canyon depths.
I take a path that is not the path

I gasp at the cliff edge.
One more step
and I would have plunged
to certain death.
Retreating, I rejoin the real path,
climb metal rungs down
to crystal pools of turquoise water
that paint the valley floor.

Temperatures bake an oppressive heat
sullen and dry
below the surface of the earth
enclosed by canyon walls.

Shimmering water curtains drop and fall.
White mists feed a cascade of dripping ferns
on sheer cliff walls.

Sandy beaches beckon,
Smooth tree arms stretch
above shallow pools.
welcoming me
to bask snakelike
along their sun-warmed bark.

But first, I plunge into a crystalline pool,
swim close to falling water as I dare,
and with gratitude to be alive,
tread water,

close eyes,
raise my hands in wonder
as water thunders all around.

☼

## 12. SEASONS

Tahuya River, Washington State, North America.

Brief seasonal notes from beside the Tahuya river:
my guide and ally for several years

### 1. Spring

Storm water recedes.
Smooth beach pebbles invite me
to learn the river's new and winding course,
after winter's wild and blustery days.

Mallards glide downstream,
pool-dabbling on their drifting way.
Upstream fronds of fir, fern,
and tooth-peeled sticks
speak of beaver work.
An unseen frog croaks nearby.

River beings return
to reclaim their watery domain
in the expanding year.

## 2. Summer

Legs immersed in cold flowing water,
fast currents wrestle taut calves.
I wade upstream,
where bright riverbed pebbles
quiver and distort like carnival mirrors.

Dark trees shadow deep-water riverbank pools.
Midstream, clouds and sky
shimmy a white/blue dance.
At shoreline, tall grass reflections.

I listen to the slosh, slurp and splash
a river-walking human makes,
while side streams trickle all around.

On a log, feet dangling,
I toss blossoms of thirty-three
wild and garden flowers
into the wandering flow
to honor a departed friend.
Tiny fishes dart to nibble
a dazzle of gliding, twirling
rainbow gifts.

The huh-woo call of a band-tailed pigeon,
flutter of an orange/brown butterfly
buzz of a honeybee sipping at the river's edge.
Fleeting moments.

## 3. Fall

Riverbank vine maples morph
from green, to orange, to fall red.
Thistledown parachutes drift
across the brightly colored stream.

First rain swells the river flow,
fills shallow ponds,
drowns shoreline beaches.
Three inches more rain and
squads of pink/dark-grey coho
leap small rapids,
fling aging bodies
toward spawning grounds.
The river celebrates
with ecstatic splash and thrash,
a water-world season of procreation.

Heavy rain now, the river an orchestra,
a swelling crescendo of racing water
sucking at river banks,
dragging loose roots and trunks
feeding a muddy foam-crested torrent.

## 4. Winter

The January river quiet
in the death-walk time of year.
With salmon bones picked clean,
an eagle pipes a shrill and reedy call
from a stripped-bare maple branch.
Water seeps and trickles through new pathways

as the logjam settles for another year.

Shallow pools freeze over,
icicles hang from water-splashed river debris,
mystical patterns of ice geometry sparkle
under a silent and clear blue winter sky.

☼

## 13. UNDER THE GLACIER

Carbon River, Mt Rainier, Washington, North America.

On a winter day
between high water of November rain
and flooding snowmelt of spring,
I wander by the Carbon River.
Birthed from a Rainier glacier
the river winds through pebble-rock beaches
while from all sides waterfalls and raindrops
splash and spray to the background whoosh of the central flow.
The trancelike soothing ambiance of water.

A water ouzel squats and bobs a comical dance.
My feet, once boot-shod, now naked
endure the icy shock of renewal by glacial melt.
Then after morning rain has ceased,
I sink, belly down, onto a sandy river beach.
Weak sun warms my back.

I ask myself,
what are my fears,

as I lie under the volcano
below Carbon glacier
by the icy water's edge?

If the mountain blew, it would take me now.
I'd be finished after moments of instinct struggle,
gasping, choking, then buried deep
under layers of mud and uprooted trees
crashing, pounding down the valley.

No one knows where I am.
I'd disappear.
I would not be found.
My bones forever under lava flows.
I'd be okay with that.
A quick and honest way to go.

## 14. UNDERWORLD

McElmo Creek, Cortez, Colorado, North America.

Why walk across a wicked cactus nest
of spike and purple hue,
where thistles wrestle knee and thigh?
"Turn back, turn back"
these spiny guardians warn in dying light.

But some enchantment beckons me to crouch
among blackened bones of brittle twigs
where rising stench of putrefaction
hovers low at the river's edge,

where mystic veils thin between the worlds,
where water shimmers
silver at the shore of night.

Undercurrents murmur:
There is no choice, there is no choice
but to sing and chant,
to slip outside familiar rooms of mind
to answer the call to leave
the dimming world behind.

Songs of river whispers
creep inside my bones
as I say YES, and YES again
in the black of night
to that which waits
unnamed beyond the light.

## 15. DOWN UNDER

Einsleigh River, Queensland, Australia

With a ticket to anywhere in the world,
there are choices,
unlimited choices of destination.

With so much freedom,
a purpose must be found or created,
a quest to be fulfilled.
With a gift that cannot be squandered,
I look to signs to show the way.

A photo whispers
from the other side of the world.
A river.
And I know it is that river,
so far away,
invisibly beckoning me
to visit the shallow river pools
and rounded basalt rocks
of a languid outback flow in the dry.

The photographer,
a soulful, kind and generous ally,
guides me to the river
on a continent never before visited.

Blue sky, cloud puffs and Australian winter sunshine
shine pristine reflections on glassy water.
The image now made alive, seen, felt,
heard and walked within,
and within me.

At that time of year
serene, silent, a quiet blue mirror
held by sandbank mounds, smooth dark basalt rocks,
paperbark and eucalyptus trees bent low.
A place for storing quiet moments.

Now, the river in a far corner of the world
Runs, light-bathed, through memory
and through my own photograph of that magical place.

☼

## 16. RIVER OF THE FUTURE

Life wanders on
toward
an unknown river flow…

# 17. Trip Back

INTRODUCTION

"Have you forgotten?" they sang,
"have you forgotten all the ways
we told you to remember?"

I had forgotten
every thought, word and feeling.

In the letting go,
my mind a clean slate,
I had drifted, plunged and wandered
into a new life
beyond memory.

EVENTUALLY, inner voices nudged me to uncover why, for so many years, my life had been a quest for a life 'beyond memory', a life lived only for the present, untouched by the past, unencumbered by desires or vision for the future. Of what use or value was the past? Indifferent to history, I disliked antiques, ruins, fashions, attitudes, anything moldering from the rust and decay of time. The present was where it was at. Only the present was important—to be as present as possible in the moment. Be Here Now. Wasn't that the goal of meditation, even enlightenment—to respond to the immediate moment with full awareness? And yes, I often experienced that balanced, in between state of 'being in the now' to a degree, and it worked. But why had I narrowed life to such a limited focus? Why had I refused to accept, perhaps honor, even appreciate, all that had gone before, all that had informed, and culminated, in the present? And what about the future? Why had I not allowed visions of a wider future than that held in check by the present? I was afraid of the past, and at the same time afraid of the future. I believed that happiness lay only in the experience of NOW.

Then, gradually, after many years, and a growing curiosity, I let myself slip from the often pleasurable and carefree restraints of the present, to explore the past, to examine the ragged tapestry of what had formed and molded me to the life I live today. First, I invited to the forefront of memory my early adult years, after I had left my country of birth to live in the United States at a turbulent time in the world. Results of that inner exploration inspired the creation of fictitious characters, settings, and scenarios in a novel. After completion of the novel, I plunged my attention deeper into the past, to childhood, school years, and toward my family of origin, of whose lives I remembered little.

The time had come to answer the questions: What were my parents to me? Who was my brother? What were the influences of my childhood? For so many years I hadn't much cared.

# WEDNESDAY

THE plane banks to the right. Sunlight flashes gold off a silvery wing before the plane begins its steady descent to Heathrow airport through a dense shroud of late February fog. My seat in upright position, my seatbelt fastened, I close my eyes and breathe through waves of anticipation and anxiety coursing through my body.

I imagine the immigration officer's questions and how I will answer.

"What is the purpose of your visit?"

"To visit relatives."

"Will you be staying with them?"

"No."

"Where do they live?"

"Brighton, Chichester, Hereford."

"Addresses? You've left that blank."

"Well, you see, they're all disembodied, interred or scattered, in the spirit world," I'll say with a straight face.

"Oh," he'll say as he stamps my visa, thinking 'harmless enough, another nut case from America looking for her roots.'

It has been twenty-four years since I visited my country of birth. Forty-six years since I called England home. Fifty years since an event I am now traveling from so far away to investigate further.

The original intention for my trip was to pay respects to my family of origin—mother, father, and brother—by visiting graves sites or cremation grounds, and to collect my mother's ashes to bring back to America to scatter off the Washington coast, a place she had loved. Not an easy task since I didn't know where those graves or ashes were. I had lost touch with the few people I knew in England, and all my parents' friends and relatives were dead. But fortunately, I had a few clues, and my memory did not entirely fail me. I knew the names of the towns where my mother, father, and brother had died.

Weeks of online investigation and numerous emails paid off better than expected. I also guessed that memories would unfold and far more would be revealed once I embarked on my journey to honor the dead.

I had occasionally wondered why I felt no love for England and chose to leave, emigrating to the United States with an American husband when scarcely out of my teens, re-inventing myself as an entirely new person in an era when transformational possibilities were limitless. At first I'd thought that leaving England stemmed from a desire for adventure and freedom prompted by the stifling atmosphere and hypocrisy of British life—and the frequent cold, gray, dreary weather.

But when I glanced even sideways at my family history, glaringly obvious answers appeared to my question: Why choose to settle so far from my native land? Nine years of oppressive boarding school had all but crushed my spirit; my only sibling, an older brother, had committed suicide with cyanide; my mother was a lesbian, long before the general acceptance of gay culture; and my father disowned me.

WHEN the pilot's voice announces that five-hundred-thousand people are in the air at that moment, I am reminded that flying is a non-event. Even though no stranger to air travel, I smile with relief to be safely back on earth when the plane touches down onto the runway at Heathrow airport with only the slightest judder.

In an early memory, on my first flight, at the age of two, from London to Gibraltar, I remember stumbling across the aisle and throwing up—not the greatest introduction to air travel, or the greatest of early memories. At seven, as a junior jet club member, I traveled unaccompanied from London to Kano in Northern Nigeria, a long, slow, noisy twenty-hour journey by propeller plane with stops in Rome and Tripoli to refuel. Since then, I've been in dozens of airports, but always held a special fondness for Heathrow, where, as a teenager, a boyfriend and I rode the tube from Central London to the airport arrivals gate and acted exaggerated 'meet and greet' scenarios, hugging and kissing after pretended long periods of separation.

The airport still holds an air of excitement for me.

Immigration is a breeze. The officer doesn't ask more than the first question, barely glances at my face, and stamps my passport, satisfied with my brief response. Too bad, I think, I would have enjoyed injecting a little levity into the solemn and cruel business of whether or not a person can enter a country. Airports are such serious business.

While I wait by the baggage carousel, I watch small stories unfold: an elegant and colorful Indian family reunites with an elderly relative recently arrived from Asia; an impeccably dressed business man, in London perhaps for a corporate deal or employment opportunity, walks purposefully toward the exit; parents herd three sleepy-eyed children through Baggage Claim, maybe on their way to visit relatives or for their first European vacation. I wonder if anyone guesses why I wander through Heathrow that day, but apart from a security guard, whose job description includes guessing the back-story and intention of every traveler, the crowd looks far too busy to notice me. Feeling like an undercover agent on a mission, I enjoy the anonymity of aloneness in the midst of a crowd.

I pick up a personal wi-fi, buy transportation passes and head to catch a tube to a Bed and Breakfast booked online before leaving the States.

Immediately, and unexpectedly, sounds and smells of the Underground station snap me back to childhood: the sour, sooty stench of dank tunnels; the monstrous roar, whoosh and screech of an approaching train; tube doors sliding open; the footsteps and shuffle of departing passengers; the recorded litany from overhead speakers of: "mind the gap"; tube doors sliding closed; then the whistling acceleration of a train pulling out of the station. The sounds and smells have not changed. Surprised and fascinated by how deeply embedded in my unconscious those sensory memories must be, they trigger no particular emotion of either fondness or fear. I hadn't thought of them since the last time I traveled by tube, many years before.

I wait for the next train on the Piccadilly line platform.

Until the age of two, I lived near the north end of the Piccadilly line in north London with my grandparents. Later, my brother and I often stayed with them on school vacations when we didn't travel to Africa to stay with our parents. Sometimes we were sent to 'holiday homes'—terrible cruel places, similar to temporary foster homes, where I remember often being treated worse than animals. Dogs had priority over the domain of armchair and couch; children sat on the floor. Far better holidays were when my mother returned to England and we occasionally rode the Piccadilly line to Central London, emerging from the underground to the bright glamour of Knightsbridge or Bond Street, a thrilling escape from the suburbs into the pulsing bright excitement of city life. But by far the best holidays were summer months in Northern Nigeria, far, far, from the Piccadilly Line and the fog and smog of postwar London—but that's another story to be told elsewhere.

On the tube, I listen to a wide-spectrum chorus of foreign voices. Passengers chat on mobile phones, read e-books, text, wear headphones, and check electronic devices. Only one or two passengers read Metro or Daily Mail newspapers. There's not a book in sight. I feel out of touch with London's international world, although the vitality, diversity, and innovation I've already seen in a short time are surprisingly energizing, despite my travel-weariness and lack of sleep.

At South Ealing, I walk two blocks to a Bed and Breakfast. Red-brick-walled houses and rows of small butcher, baker, and grocer shops feel familiar despite the many years since I walked the streets of London. When I reach the Bed and Breakfast, I marvel again how International London has become. The owner, Benny, is from Iraq, and the Manager, Asanthi, from Sri Lanka. Over the reception desk a sign reads: "Change is not death. Fear of change is death."

I wonder if I am ready for whatever changes, challenges and insights the trip might bring.

All evening I sleep soundly but at two in the morning I'm fully awake with a scrambled body clock. I plug in my wi-fi and go online. Almost immediately a Skype call comes in from a friend in Western Australia who thinks I'm in Northwest USA. Within minutes an email pops up from India, and another from an island in Puget Sound. Now I no longer feel the slightest bit out of touch; I am my own international hub, currently based in London.

☼

# THURSDAY

I DEDICATE today to my mother.

Swerving and ducking through swarms of incoming early morning commuters at Victoria Station, I head toward the platform for the Brighton train. Men and women rush with single-minded focus to city offices as if arriving late is a sin with severe repercussions—exactly as I remember. But the station feels busier, lighter, brighter and cleaner. Digitally streamlined arrival and departure boards hang high over the hall above the platforms, replacing the click of the old roll-over information boards. The price of using the public toilets has risen dramatically, now far more expensive than 'spending a penny', and the queues longer; pungent citrus smells have replaced the stink of Lysol disinfectant, which wouldn't be so bad except for the certainty the strong citrus scents are also probably carcinogenic.

The high-speed train pulls away from the station, gathers speed, shimmies and jerks from side to side, rushes past long forgotten, and now familiar, row after row of chimneyed brick houses beside the rail lines. Washing, hung to dry in small grimy backyards, flaps in the breeze. I feel comforted knowing many things haven't changed in my years away. Stations flash by: East Croydon, Gatwick Airport, Haywards Heath.

The train to Brighton, where I plan to visit my mother's ashes, will pass close by my first boarding school in Haywards Heath, or "'aywards 'eath, 'aywards 'eath," as the train conductor announced when I was a child—Haywards Heath, the town where I spent seven of nine years at boarding school.

Most boarding school horrors you've read about or seen in movies are true. My own memories of various clichéd scenarios come flooding back. I'll spare you the worst of them.

☼

A NEW school term began at Victoria Station crowded with noisy clusters of girls from different boarding schools milling around on adjacent platforms, each group wearing their specific brand of uniform—hats, ties and blazers—with maroon, navy blue, dark green and gray the predominant colors. Stacks of school trunks and suitcases lined platforms ready for an army of porters to load them into luggage compartments. During those school years I packed and unpacked school trunks fifty-four times—six times a year for nine years. No wonder I'm good at packing for travel.

My stoic mother said an awkward goodbye to her equally stoic daughter at the platform with a quick hug and held-back tears. I didn't cry or cling to my mother like many of the other students. The first time I caught the school train I remember anticipating my new adventure with great excitement; after all, my big brother, who had already been at boarding school for two years, wore a compelling aura of sophistication around me and I figured it must have been the result of boarding school.

It didn't take long for the excitement to vanish. An early school memory: once a week we wrote a letter home. I quickly learned those unsealed letters were read, and heavily censored. I had written to my mother, telling her tearfully how meanly I'd been teased by dorm-mates, and how unhappy I was. The headmistress summoned me to her study and held up the unsent letter. I received no sympathy from her. Under her stern, unsympathetic eye, I wept again while re-writing the letter to pass inspection: "Dear Mummy, I am well. How are you? School is nice. I learn a lot in my lessons. Love, Linda." We might as well have sent home standard form letters.

After an initial period of rebellion, I learned to choke back tears, accept and surrender to my new life. Weren't all the other girls at school in the same situation? We all survived as best we could. I learned resilient independence so I could survive in the face of adversity.

Almost all my current friends can recall the names of at least several classmates from school days. I remember only two full names, and those were from my earliest year of boarding school at the age of seven; both friends were already out of my life by the time I was eight. That was it. Two names out of nine years of school; plus the first name of a friend who named a pet chicken after me. I remember no faces. I have no photographs. Both boarding schools closed within two years of my leaving. No old school friends have tried to reconnect with me on Facebook. Or perhaps they have, but they wouldn't have found me—I've had three different first and last names.

Why didn't I remember? Did I remember the names of friends at one time, and later erased them? Had I become so withdrawn and hidden, like an earthworm living safely in its subterranean world, and everything else was unimportant? Or was I so engrossed in living in the interiority of my own being that my mind considered outside information irrelevant? Perhaps during my school years I slipped slowly into a gray area for self-preservation, and slowly deadened myself to outside interaction. For a while, my nickname was 'Smug'. Perhaps the nickname summed it up. I kept to myself, often with a half-smile to hide my sensitivity. For several years, half the time I was in a classroom two years ahead of my age group, and the other half I spent in dormitories where girls my age enjoyed fewer privileges than my classmates.

I do remember teachers' names. Maybe the teachers were more important to me than the other girls, and left a lasting impression. More than their names, I remember them as cartoonlike caricatures: the tall skinny matron with chin hairs, a wart, and two thin greasy gray/black braids tied around her head; the ancient, dreamy, Latin and Literature teacher who

110

slumped back in her chair and gazed trancelike out of a window in an imaginary world of her own, oblivious to her students, then snapped back into the room, leapt up, shouted, spluttered, and threw chalk; the voluptuous soft-spoken music teacher; the well-muscled, no-nonsense, short-haired gym teacher; the diminutive, gray-haired, beady-eyed headmistress with a neat bun on top of her head who taught math, and her deep-voiced girlfriend who coached lacrosse and netball. My favorite was the ancient, dreamy, otherworldly Latin and Literature teacher.

Content enough in my own little world, not particularly disliked, even as the nerdy girl with glasses, I fitted in as best I could, while attempting to stay out of trouble. I learned the safety of keeping quiet, completing schoolwork, and avoiding situations resulting in harsh repercussions. I was not always successful though at staying out of trouble—'talking after lights out' being the frequent cause of draconian punishment far outweighing the crime. For an offense I don't recall, perhaps for speaking out against some indignity, being 'cheeky' or, as was often the case, for 'talking after lights out', I was condemned for weeks to a dormitory of older girls who had been ordered to 'send her to Coventry', a old English term meaning to deliberately ostracize someone. They were never to speak to me, and to ignore me as if I didn't exist. Nothing makes a child feel smaller than feeling they do not exist. Another time, I was sent to live in the sick ward for grumbling; I wasn't sick. Isolated, I retreated into myself, slowly growing quieter and quieter, while at mealtimes I stuffed myself with greater and greater quantities of thick white bread coated with greasy margarine and sweet generic jam, washed down by cups of sweet watery tea.

But all was not dismal. I lived for Sunday walks to woodlands and fields, especially on summer days when we rested in tall grass looking up through wildflowers and waving grass-heads in a place we called Paradise. In spring we visited shady primrose and bluebell woods. I tended my own three-by-six foot flowerbed, put on plays with friends in bushy clearings on the school grounds, escaped for midnight swims at the neighboring boys' school swimming pool narrowly missing expulsion, ran away at the age of nine, again narrowly missing expulsion, made art, and spent hours burrowed in the school library.

Many years later, the last job my mother held was as a matron at a girl's boarding school. I wonder if perhaps it was repayment of karmic debt for the years her children suffered at boarding schools. I'm sure she was far kinder than the matron I remember.

The train races on from Haywards Heath to Brighton Station.

AFTER nine years of boarding school, from the age of sixteen to eighteen, I lived for two years with my mother in Seaford on the south coast of England. But, hungry to experience the world, how could I be interested in life at home when nearby Brighton captured my youthful attention? In the 1960s, Brighton was a teenager's dream—an exciting place at an exciting time. While gangs of mods and rockers battled on the beaches, I aligned with beatnik poets, folksingers, art students and alcohol—a combination that led to failing all my University entrance exams except for a pass mark in Geography. My wise mother never denied me the freedom I desperately needed after years of girls-only boarding schools. I was grateful for that. My days with like-minded students at Brighton Tech, and nights at clubs and pubs, won over any desire for family life, which I had hardly known anyway. At the same time, driving home late at night along the coastal road to Seaford, often through dense fog, and often tipsy, I looked forward to the safety of my cozy room on the top floor of my mother's house with a window facing toward the sea.

GROWING up, how little I knew about my mother, and even less about the dynamics of close-knit family life. Even in my happiest childhood years, from the age of two to six, on the rock of Gibraltar, I was often lovingly cared for by a Spanish nanny.

My mother, Audrey, met my father, Maurice, through one of her close friends, Monica, after my father had recently accepted an offer of a career opening in West Africa. Monica had been engaged to marry Maurice, but when she heard he had accepted an overseas position, she broke off the engagement, saying she didn't want to live abroad and have children who would then be sent away to boarding school. Heartbroken, Maurice left for West Africa alone. Audrey and Maurice, who had known each other only briefly for a week through Monica, began a correspondence lasting a year before she joined him in Ghana (then the Gold Coast), where they married. Audrey did not share Monica's concerns about sending her children away to boarding school. I also suspect my adventurous mother wanted to escape the boring confines of the London suburb where she lived with her strict Victorian parents.

Before marrying my father, my mother had had an affair with a woman. My father knew about it. Years later, long after my parent's divorce, he complained bitterly to me that my mother, knowing she was gay, should never have married him.

I wondered if my mother's lover had been my mother's close friend Monica, previously engaged to my father, and who remained a lifelong friend of the family.

While I was away in boarding school, during their years in West Africa, my parents lived a freewheeling colonial life of parties, alcohol and wife-swapping, but with a twist. My mother, rather than succumb to pressure from my father to sleep with other men, told me years later she preferred to seduce their bored colonial wives. On vacations in France, without their children, my parents visited the same Parisian whorehouses. They smoked kief in Morocco—perhaps in the same promiscuous ex-pat circles as author Paul Bowles. Sending their children away to school enabled them to preserve the veneer of a traditional marriage whenever we spent time together as a family. My parents stayed married for as long as they did, 'for the children'.

I WAS seventeen before I realized my mother was gay, a year after my parents' divorce and my brother's suicide.

"Your mother's really butch," a boyfriend had said bluntly.

"What do you mean?"

"You know, gay, queer, lesbian, a dyke. Just watch how she is with her friends."

I had either been mind-numbingly unobservant, or hadn't understood the significance of my mother's relationships outside her marriage to my father. I don't remember being particularly upset, only surprised. The preceding year had been full of shocks.

How could I not have known?

I WAS a young teenager when my mother bought a house in Seaford to be closer to her children, and also close to her own mother in a nearby assisted living facility, not far from where I spent my last two years of boarding school—two far better years than the first seven, although I don't remember the names of any of the girls from that school either. Soon after buying the house, a friend of my mother, Shirley, rented a room. I liked Shirley: a tall, upbeat, practical woman with an easy laugh who had been a nurse. It never occurred to me that they were lovers; it only became obvious after my boyfriend enlightened me.

Knowing my mother was gay explained the eccentric women, 'aunts', friends with my mother over the years—in particular, 'Auntie Greta' a short, muscular, leather-clad woman with a broad Yorkshire accent who had been a motorcycle dispatch rider during the Second World War and who later ran a car delivery service. I still remember driving tips shared by Auntie Greta when she taught me to drive. Another 'aunt' was a South African music teacher.

The subject of my mother being a lesbian never surfaced while I lived in her house. I wasn't a teenager who asked questions, or even initiated conversations. My school years had excelled at teaching me silence. My mother being a lesbian wasn't important; also, she must have thought she hid her gayness from me.

After leaving home, I lived in London for eighteen months, and then moved to Greece. My mother came to visit me in Athens. The evening she arrived, she took me out to dinner, drank several glasses of wine, and encouraged me to do the same as we slowly ate our moussaka. She fidgeted nervously, obviously hoping the wine would give her courage for some serious sharing. I didn't need to ask what she wanted to talk about. I had already guessed.

I entertained her with small talk about my life in Greece and waited for her to begin the real conversation.

"I have something I have to tell you," she said finally, hesitating, biting her lip. "I'm gay."

"It's okay Mom. I know. I've known for a long time." It really was okay.

My mother added tearfully that her girlfriend Shirley had left her. Shirley had moved to Ireland to become a nun and repent her 'sins.'

AFTER my mother's cremation in 1980, the staff at the crematorium said her ashes would be boxed and stored until claimed. Then I left for India. After subsequent adventures when I literally let go of almost all my past—including paperwork, memories, photographs, possessions and nationality—I no longer remembered exactly where those ashes were, only that they were stored at a cemetery in Brighton.

Thirty years later, on my current trip to England, I planned to collect my mother's ashes and bring them to the States to scatter in the Pacific Ocean close to where we had shared a peaceful vacation shortly before her death. Finally ready to claim the box containing her ashes, through an online search, I discovered the location of the cemetery where they were stored. I should not have been surprised to learn through email that the ashes had been unceremoniously tossed out years before in the crematorium scatter-ground. After her cremation it never occurred to me to inquire if boxed ashes had a shelf-life expiration date. Now I know.

Leaving the bustle of Brighton Station behind, I catch the 37B bus to the crematorium. As the bus drives through Old

116

Steine and winds up narrow streets lined with prettily painted row houses, I recall sites of teenage adventures: wild dancing at the underground Chinese Jazz Club on Brighton waterfront; a friend's basement flat on Old Steine Road where I gave my virginity to a barefoot beat poet/photography student; and I smile as I pass the home of a much-older rascal of a boyfriend, Mick the Spiv.

At the Downs crematorium, near the bottom of a long winding driveway, the friendly head gardener pulls over in his utility vehicle and gives me a ride uphill through acres of weathered gravestones to a section at the top of a grassy slope where my mother's ashes were scattered.

From the top of the quiet hillside, a panoramic view stretches for miles across the South Downs and Brighton to the English Channel.

For an early spring day, the weather is surprisingly pleasant and mild. Sunshine warms a fresh blue-sky morning. Intricate birdsong drifts over the peaceful hillside. Toward the end of her life, my mother took up bird watching and would have identified the birds who sing this morning's sweet melodies.

I rest on a bench overlooking the slope and relax deeply into the quiet, my back leaning against an old pebble flint wall. Unexpected, yet welcome tears of happiness spill down my cheeks from the overwhelming peace and beauty of the scene. Bright clumps of daffodils, snowdrops, primroses, hyacinth and crocus spring haphazardly from young grass; colorful bouquets of freshly cut flowers decorate small memorials. The abundance and beauty of blossoms blooming at the scatter ground are a fitting tribute to my mother and her love of flowers.

I remember the elegant, exquisite, and often exotic, flower arrangements filling my mother's home in Seaford. For several years she worked as a floral designer, creating artistic displays for churches and society events, including the royal wedding of the Queen's sister, Princess Margaret, and for a while owned a flower business delivering weekly bouquets to tenants of apartment buildings.

Below the slope of the scatter ground, a subdued group enters a chapel to witness the cremation of a loved one. At my mother's cremation, the only mourners were women.

I think of how, during her lifetime, few people saw my mother for her true self. Perhaps to compensate, she worked for years at a home for blind ex-service men, many of whom had not only lost their sight, but also speech and hearing, their only communication being through sign language from hand to hand. My mother became their eyes, their ears and voice by signing with touch when she escorted the men to horse races, to movies, and to the opera, and accompanied one blind/deaf man on a cruise to South Africa.

WHEN news arrived that my mother's terminal cancer had progressed and she neared the end of her life at too young of an age, I traveled back to England with my son to care for her so she could die at her home. I knew she would not want to spend her remaining days in a hospital hooked up to tubes and die surrounded by strangers. Having heard stories of caring for someone dying of cancer, and how long-drawn-out and challenging an ordeal it could be, I planned and prepared to stay for six months or longer.

The day after I had arrived at my mother's cottage in Seaford, she returned home after staying with her current girlfriend, Sonya, in the north of England for a week. She walked in the door looking fragile, but well. Two weeks later, she was dead. Shockingly swift, the end came much, much faster than expected. It seemed as if, as soon as we had arrived, she knew her daughter and grandson were thriving, and she felt safe to let go and leave the world with the minimum of fuss. A week after my arrival, immediately after returning home from a visit to her lawyer to amend her will, my mother's mind began to slip. She had finished what she felt necessary to complete her time on earth. After that, I watched, amazed, and shocked, as my mother's body entered daily accelerating cycles of clutching desperately to life, then letting go, until the final spiral of rapid wasting when a thin layer of parchment-like skin barely stretched over her bones. With the stoicism I had witnessed before, my mother would take only one pain pill while enduring her shockingly swift and painful process of dying, letting go, and leaving the sorrows of her life behind.

After slipping into a coma the morning before her death, my mother visited me in an ecstatic inner vision, peaceful and ready to leave the world, telling me she would have left earlier had she known before what she felt at that moment—the euphoric experience of floating freely in the radiant glow of a light-filled world of bliss consciousness. I psychically told her to hold on a few more hours until Sonya arrived that evening from the north of England; I knew her girlfriend would want to say goodbye. My mother waited. Early the following morning she left her body, flooding the house for hours with the same luminescent brilliance she had communicated to me psychically the previous day.

During the short intense time of caring for my mother before her transition, I felt a completion in our relationship, with loving and kind goodbyes, both verbal and non-verbal, accompanied by silent prayers and mantras. My only regret was I had not spent more time with my mother, and known how to love and care for her more, when she was living.

I RISE slowly from the bench by the cemetery wall, then kneel on the tender spring grass between a patch of snowdrops and daffodils and place my palms against the earth. I lower my head to the ground to honor the loving memory of my mother.

Inside the rich soil, my mother's ashes have crumbled and dissolved to feed new generations of life. My mother's voice is heard in all the sweet notes of birdsong, and her beauty is seen in every bright flower and blade of grass on that peaceful springtime hillside.

☼

STILL early in the afternoon, back at Brighton station, I check train times to London, and then spontaneously change my mind and catch a slow train to Seaford to visit my mother's house where I stayed when not in boarding school. My original trip planning hadn't included a visit to my teenage home; I'd thought I would only visit cemeteries.

On the train, small country stations stir pleasant memories: London Road, Falmer, Lewes, Southease, Newhaven Town, Newhaven Harbor, Bishopstone, Seaford; for my last two years at home I traveled daily from Seaford to school in Brighton, gazing dreamily out the windows at peaceful rural scenes. Today I look out across the wide flat valley of the winding River Ouse and green rolling hills of the South Downs remembering long walks along well-trodden paths with my mother and her cairn terrier.

Seaford has changed little from the sleepy seaside town I remember. As I leave the train station the smell of the sea air rushes to greet me. A gull cries overhead. I walk slowly down a narrow street past an old stone church, past a pub and a café whose names have remained unchanged for more than fifty years, past the 17<sup>th</sup> century cottage where my mother spent the last years of her life, to the corner house where I lived as a teenager when I wasn't either in Africa or boarding school— the house where my mother and I received the news of my brother's death.

ON a quiet Sunday morning, April 1<sup>st</sup>, April Fools' Day, after visiting my grandparents in north London, my mother and I arrived back at our south coast home. As I turned the handle of the front door, I heard the phone ring on the second floor. I ran in, leapt upstairs and answered the call, surprised to hear my grandfather's voice since we had so recently left his house. "Put your mother on the phone," he said with unfamiliar urgency.

Feeling something was terribly wrong, I ran downstairs and told my mother to hurry to the phone. Perhaps my grandmother had passed away, although she had been full of life when we left her house only hours before. From the bottom of the staircase I faintly heard my mother's side of the conversation. "NO! An accident? …ill?" Something *was* terribly wrong. My grandmother must have had an accident. My mother closed the door and continued her conversation.

Minutes later, my mother opened the door, leaned over the banisters and said softly and slowly, with a shaky voice, "Linda, you have to be brave. Christopher has died."

NO! How could that be? I collapsed, sobbing, at the kitchen table. I couldn't speak.

"He had a burst appendix."

Was this some kind of sick April Fools' joke?

In the following days, in a blur of shock, although sensing something more to Christopher's death than the burst appendix story, in my usual way of keeping quiet, I didn't say a word. A month went by before I summoned the courage to ask my mother if she had told me the truth about his death. She bit her lip, blinked back tears, took a deep breath and admitted she had been trying to protect me from the truth; my brother had taken his life because he was depressed. I didn't want to upset my mother further with questions. Months later I learned vague hints: an older woman, an artist, had been involved; Christopher had left a note; he had died from cyanide poisoning. That was the last of it. I asked no more questions, silently witnessing my mother's sorrow, and going through my own process of grieving.

I didn't go to Christopher's funeral. To lessen my shock and grief, my mother sent me to stay with my grandparents before returning for my last few months of boarding school. My father flew back from Africa for the funeral. I didn't see my father, and never asked either of them where the funeral service and burial were held. It never occurred to me to find out where he was buried and to visit his grave until fifty years later.

I WANDER along the Seaford waterfront. The town might not have changed, but the seafront has. A million tons of dredged up pebbles have been trucked in to raise the beach more than twenty feet to meet the sea wall in what must have been a huge, lengthy and expensive operation; shady breakwaters are gone; concrete steps to the beach have disappeared, and a long unbroken stretch of gently sloping shoreline almost reaches the promenade. Beside the walkway to the chalky cliffs of Seaford Head, previously shabby, storm-battered rows of beach huts now look like a spring garden, newly painted with fresh pastel colors. On this fine weather day, fast walkers, joggers and strollers crowd the esplanade. I remember windswept January days when I was the only person out in such stormy weather, wandering along the seafront, reveling in white sheets of spray that leapt the sea wall and soaked my clothes.

I look into the faces of people my age and wonder if they have lived in this town their whole lives. Or like me, have they returned after many years, to stoke memories, gain insights, and, I admit, even to indulge a hint of nostalgia.

Many happy teenage hours passed on Seaford beach, despite its steep slope of hard pebbles, cold rough water and rare sunny days. I hung out here with my first boyfriend, launched his tiny wooden boat, Matchbox, and rowed through choppy Channel waves, swam, played and laughed; where my friends and I spent hours chatting and flirting; and where I picnicked with my mother and brother in the shelter of wave-worn breakwaters.

I know I made the right decision to take the side trip to Seaford.

Everywhere birds sing loudly, celebrating springtime. Back at Seaford station, a crowd of seagulls squabble over a scrap of discarded pastry on the platform while I wait for the London train. When the train stops at Lewes station, I see noisy crows have built multiple nests in a stand of trees. Everywhere, complex warbler song-lines keep me grounded in the present time.

I chat easily with another passenger on the train, something I would never have done when I lived in England. Growing up, I didn't talk to strangers. Today I do. I have grown curious about people: who they are; their lives, ideas, experiences; their way of being in the world. I ask questions. I learn from others. I have lost most of my British shyness, while staying sensitive to the need for boundaries. By sharing stories—my less dramatic ones—others open up with their own unique stories. This seems especially true in England.

At Victoria Station I wrestle against the tide of late rush hour crowds leaving the city.

A familiar face approaches and passes me by. I can't figure out where I've seen him. I turn around, curious, and follow him. I overtake and recognize him immediately. What amazing synchronicity! Out of all the millions of people in London, I run into a friend, my car mechanic from Seattle who, years before, had also chosen to leave England for the States. He's in London for a week visiting friends and is as surprised and delighted as I am to cross paths with someone he knows from halfway around the world. He invites me to join him for an evening with his friends, but I decline. It's been a long day.

On the way to my Bed and Breakfast in South Ealing, when changing trains on the Underground, I fail to check whether the sign on the train reads North Ealing or South Ealing. I ask another passenger if this is the right train for South Ealing. "No," he says, "this one's for North Ealing. You have to get off at the next stop and catch the right one." I get ready to change trains, but in less than a minute there's an announcement over the loud speaker: "Due to a signal failure, this train has been diverted to the South Ealing route. All passengers bound for North Ealing must change at the next station." Everyone gets off the train except me. What luck!

The warm spring day has gifted me generously with memories and magical moments.

# FRIDAY

FRIDAY is the first of two days I have set aside for my father, Maurice.

The tube, jammed with commuters, squeals, rumbles and roars through tunnels to Victoria Station in the morning rush hour. The scene feels science fiction-like with crowds of silent people, crammed-together, speeding through the earth in metal containers. Standing passengers lean backwards and forwards in unison, then to the left and to the right, swaying in waves to the rhythm of the rocking train; I hold tight to a pole to keep my balance. When a man offers me a seat, I know I must look old, although I don't feel old. I like to think jet lag must have suddenly aged me. I accept the offer.

The train route from Victoria to Chichester travels through idyllic farm and country scenes: greening hedgerows, budding trees, and early spring fields birthing a first hint of early green against rich brown soil. A light fog adds an air of mystery to the cool morning. Crawley, Horsham, Pulborough. Above a misty hillside, Arundel Castle towers over the town of Arundel. The last time I saw my father was in Arundel, where he lived until the end of his life with Maureen, his second wife.

I loved my father. I also realize I had mistakenly entertained an idealized faith or belief that underneath—or above—it all, he had loved me as I loved him, despite our inability to communicate in the everyday world, in addition to his physical absence for most of my life. A belief probably common to many with absent fathers.

An astrologer, who knew nothing about me except for what he saw from my birth date, asked me once: "How is your relationship with your father."

"Good," I replied.

He raised his eyebrows. "Really?"

125

I had seen my father twice in thirty-three years. Both times ended in disaster. What an incredible disconnect between the reality and my belief!

Even after events triggered my father to tell me he wanted no further contact, I continued to send him a yearly Christmas card, receiving nothing in return. I also wrote a respectful, conciliatory letter to his second wife, Maureen, who had played a major role in our separation. In the letter I asked my stepmother to let me know if my father fell ill or died. She didn't reply. Years later, around New Year, I received a letter from Maureen thanking me for the recent yearly Christmas card. And saying my father had died of lung cancer nine months previously, in March. Immediately, tears flooded my eyes, and then right behind, anger flared toward Maureen. Along with the anger arose the thought my father *must* have loved his daughter, but had fallen prey to Maureen—a weak man under the spell of a jealous, vindictive wife. As the victim of a real-life wicked stepmother drama, I had, more than once, described Maureen to friends as a 'psychotic bitch'.

Perhaps though, I knew deep down, despite Maureen, my father and I would never have overcome our differences: blame of my mother for her sexuality and the suicide of his only son; my rebellion against his way of life; his dislike of my choice to marry an American, move to the United States and become an American citizen. Although his aversion to my marriage choice and move to America was probably influenced by Maureen's narrow-minded xenophobic views.

An ambitious man, my father grew up poor in Hackney, at that time slums of London, the son of a greengrocer. He worked hard to improve his status through education and as a social climber. And, mostly, he succeeded.

My grandfather on my mother's side was a successful banker, manager of the Midland Bank in the City of London, and his father, my great grandfather, had been a silk merchant in Shanghai. My mother grew up higher up the social ladder than Maurice, though not quite 'upper class'. A red-headed beauty, theatrical and witty, she trained to go on the stage to act in musical comedy, although never pursued it as a career due to health issues. My mother's family tree dates back to 1600, with the first name John Hope. Hope has been carried down either as last or middle name since then. Had Maurice married my mother for a rise in status? If so, he hadn't bargained on later suffering with coming to terms with her sexual preference. He poured his energy into his work, ending up with a shattered family: his first wife failed him; the suicide of his son devastated him; his daughter left her country of birth and became a hippie.

With determination, understated charisma and quiet wit, my father charmed his way upward, but he never attained exactly the right accent for the 'old boys club' with an 'in' to the best jobs. He had to work twice as hard, and the stigma of his background never completely vanished. He won a scholarship to Cambridge University, where he excelled, but didn't rise all the way to the top. As a mathematics whiz, he earned good advanced degrees, but not the best; although he rowed for Cambridge for two years, he failed to row in the most prestigious race, the Oxford/Cambridge boat race.

At the time my father was an undergraduate, Cambridge was renowned for recruitment of bright young men as 'spies' for KGB, or for enlistment for secret government work in the years before the Second World War. Had he perhaps been enlisted? Sometimes I'd had my suspicions—but if he had been, he never ranked high in any spying world. But what did I know? He was capable of great inscrutability, and I didn't ask.

Everyone has questions they'd like to ask their parents, even long after their death. Especially, if, like me, they had so little curiosity while their parents were alive. For many years, absorbed in patching my own life together and attempting to understand the process, there was little room for inquiry into the lives of others. I also hadn't learned a vocabulary for healthy communication about emotions until well into my adult years.

After leaving Cambridge my father accepted a colonial position in Ghana, where upper class accents were unimportant unless one aspired to the Governor's Mansion. Although he joined the British army in West Africa when the Second World War broke out in 1939, there probably wasn't much spying in that corner of the world.

After the war, my father spent time in London, took a post in Gibraltar for four years and then served ten years in Northern Nigeria, retiring from the British Colonial Service after Nigeria gained independence. The British Government awarded him the prestigious honor of a CBE (Commander of the British Empire) for services to the British Empire, second only to a knighthood. I accompanied him to Buckingham Palace when he received the CBE medal from the Queen Mother. At the event, I don't remember feeling especially proud of my father, but far more entertained and impressed by the royal glamour and theatricality of costumed musicians and liverymen. Years of boarding school had left me self-absorbed, cynical, and unresponsive to my father's achievements.

After leaving Nigeria, the death of his son, and divorce from my mother, my father remarried and returned to Africa to work on settlement schemes in Kenya for several years. He built a house for himself and his second wife, Maureen, in southern Spain, then received an appointment to the Panel of Fiscal Experts for the International Monetary Fund, accepting extended assignments in Sierra Leone, the Sudan and Zambia, with trips to check in with headquarters in Washington DC. He

128

spent his life working for an imperialistic model—causing Third World countries to be indebted to, and openly or secretly run by, powers greater than themselves, while their resources were pillaged. His last boss was Henry Kissinger.

He told me once he believed in helping Africans become educated so they could take over and run their own countries well. Despite his belief, Nigeria later became one of the most corrupt countries in the world. He also told me his commitment to me was to pay for my education. However, after nine years of boarding school, at the age of sixteen, and after my brother's suicide, I lost all interest in conventional education, and only passed the GED when almost fifty years old. Although grateful for the education I did receive, formal education in itself is not enough without the balance of a consistent, healthy, happy home life.

In my twenties, pregnant, and on my own with nowhere to live, I asked my father for a small loan to purchase a trailer. He refused. He told me the interest would be so high that I wouldn't be able to pay him back. My mother gave me the money. Many years later, after filing for a bankruptcy brought on by a combination of bad luck and foolish choices, I realized how I had internalized my father's words about paying back interest. His words had become a self-fulfilling prophecy.

IN January, before my trip to England, after two weeks of emails to unresponsive lawyers, to a distant relative of Maureen, and to two crematoriums, I received word of where my father's ashes could be found.

When I step off the train into a damp, foggy day in Chichester, there are no energetic bustling crowds as in London, or even Brighton. The people in Chichester seem older, slower, duller, less concerned with appearance, and less healthy than those in London—the English I remember.

Outside the train station I catch a bus to Chichester Crematorium. I love how easy public transportation is in England.

Despite the chilly day, as I walk through the cemetery, the air vibrates with birdsong eerily similar to birdsong heard the day before at Brighton cemetery. How strange. Are specific types of birds attracted to graveyards and sing sweetly to liven up the spirits of the dead and those who come to visit? Perhaps the birds prefer a quiet environment, away from the bustle of a city? Or, do cemeteries play recorded birdsong to create a pleasing atmosphere for visitors? The latter doesn't seem too farfetched. But perhaps I am being cynical.

Walking past grave sites, I read tombstone inscriptions: "sadly missed by all"; "you will be forever in our hearts"; "a true gentleman, a wonderful husband, Dad, Granddad and brother." Sadly, not words I would choose to describe my father. He did little for a half-sister who lived close to poverty. Ironically, his half-sister left me a small inheritance, but left nothing for her half-brother.

After so long, am I ready to forgive my father for not being present for me? After years of inner work, could there be any blame left for how the past affected my life? This foggy day, I hope here, at his final resting place, a moment of happy completion and forgiveness might arise, or at least compassionate understanding. After all, there must be some benefit to my years of believing I loved my father and that he loved me.

The deserted scatter ground lies, like an afterthought, off to the side and to the back of the cemetery, a humble place where paupers might have been buried in former times. I sit on a weather-beaten bench by a stone koi pond and listen to a trickle of water drip eerily from a small waterfall. A cold breeze blows. I shiver. The place feels gloomy, depressing and severe.

The scatter grounds occupy a shallow dip, with no sweeping panoramic views. Wilted winter leaves hang from bushes. There are no grave stones, no individually marked areas separating one person's ashes from any other; everyone is blended together anonymously in a great mixing of remains. In the letter telling me of my father's death, Maureen said he had wanted anonymity in death, and a simple, no fuss cremation. As a lifelong atheist, this humble setting would have pleased him.

In these desolate surroundings I think back to the curse placed on my father and his family. Although I never knew the wording or exact substance of the curse, I had heard that a curse, if strong enough, could be passed down for seven generations. Maybe it was all superstition. Maybe not. I guessed a spell cast by an African juju man would be powerful.

I learned of the curse the last time I visited Nigeria when I was sixteen. The family's faithful servant for many years, Ali, had suddenly packed up his family and disappeared a few months before my arrival. I asked my mother if she knew why he left. She told me he said my father had been cursed, and he was afraid. He didn't want to stay to see the fallout and the possibility of his own family being affected. As usual, I didn't ask further questions, but did wonder whether Ali was involved. Who had cast a spell on our family, and why? Perhaps an African held a grudge against my father for an injustice, either perceived or real? Perhaps antagonism toward White oppression and colonization surfaced and left my father an open target for a primitive, and often effective, form of aggression? At least he hadn't been murdered in his bed by machete, the fate of several Whites in a Kenyan uprising during the same period.

Results of the curse came soon after Ali's departure, with Christopher's suicide. Whoever had placed the curse probably knew the way to destroy a person (in this case, my father) was for something unthinkable to happen to a loved one, with the recipient of the curse continuing to live with ongoing guilt and grief. Far better than killing someone outright would be for them to suffer through blame over the loss of a family member.

I'm sure my father did suffer terribly, although we never spoke about it, and I never saw him affected emotionally—he was always difficult to 'read'. We had so little communication; he never expressed or shared his thoughts and emotions with me. How could he not have suffered? All of his ambitions had been pinned on his only son.

Several years before this trip to England I spent time with a shamanic healer who worked with removing curses and spells and I distinctly felt healing benefits from his work. Something shifted.

I wrap my scarf higher against my chin and remember the last two times I saw my father.

I arrived in southern Spain at the beginning of 1970, excited to build an adult relationship with my father and to get to know my stepmother, Maureen, whom I had previously met only briefly. I had planned on staying in Spain for a couple of weeks, having recently split up from a short marriage to my American husband and deciding whether to continue living in the United States or return to Europe. Maurice and Maureen met me at the airport. On the drive to their newly built home in Torreblanca in southern Spain, Maureen, a staunch Catholic, turned to me in the back seat and stated imperiously: "I've told everyone you're my daughter. I don't want anyone to know your father has been divorced." Red flag. Why would someone, who hadn't seen her 'daughter' in a while, have me sit in the back seat and not say another word to me the rest of the ride to their home? My father remained silent.

My disastrous Spanish visit lasted two days. Before meeting my father, Maureen, a 'career woman' with a successful private medical practice on Harley Street in London, had never married and had no children. She was a fifty year old spinster who believed in 'proper' old school British etiquette and manners. I should have known Maureen would have trouble relating to me after I'd been living in a laid-back hippie community in the Rocky Mountains.

Maureen wouldn't allow me into her kitchen, put on a fussy show of how well she fed and took care of Maurice, and stepped nervously around me. I could feel a mass of tension building under her brittle veneer of politeness. The second evening, after dinner, she snapped. With explosive rage Maureen ranted and screamed at me, while I cowered, sobbing, in a corner of the couch. Her tirade was so sudden and unexpected that, in my vulnerability, I was unable to respond. My father sat in an armchair opposite, his mouth open in amazement, but didn't say a word to stem Maureen's violent outburst. I escaped to my room, wishing there was a lock on the door, paranoid she might rush in at any moment with a kitchen knife. For the next hour I listened to Maureen raging, and my father arguing, but couldn't hear their words. Maureen then marched into my room without knocking and announced her only option was to leave after what had transpired that evening. From then on, she said, I must stay and care for my father. I didn't know what to say.

I slept little, listening to the sound of my father and Maureen arguing and talking all night long. At first light, my father drove me silently to the airport. I left on the earliest morning flight back to England to stay with my mother. So much for an adult relationship with my father.

After such a fateful visit, in the years between 1970 and

1988, I corresponded irregularly with my father, usually in December when I sent a Christmas card, and he mailed me a twenty dollar bill with brief, polite news. Even though he often traveled to Washington DC for his work with the IMF and I invited him to visit and meet his grandson, he never did; there was always an excuse for not accepting my invitation.

I last saw Maurice and Maureen in November of 1988. After a good financial year, I wrote to my father saying I would like to visit them at their home in Arundel, so they could meet my son, Aaron. It was long overdue for him to meet his grandfather.

They didn't say no. Aaron and I flew to London and caught the train to Arundel. My father met us at the station and drove us to their home beside the River Arun. Aaron was on his best behavior. He had taken great effort to look well-groomed in black jeans, a gray button-down shirt, a tweed sports coat, and with his shoulder length red hair neatly combed and tied back.

While Maureen fixed a meal, my father—by then a computer whiz—intrigued Aaron with mathematical computer games and puzzles he had created and published on the internet. At dinner everyone behaved well; politeness and small talk ruled, although Maureen frequently belittled Maurice with snide remarks that he was her favorite pet 'dog.' Inwardly, I cringed. My father, with downcast eyes, said nothing to defend himself. Over the years they must have settled into a pattern of verbal abuse; I could hardly believe what I heard. Maureen dominated the conversation, with talk of British TV shows I had never heard of, British politics, and her opinionated dislike of America, Americans, and foreigners in general, always with a hypocritical smile. Aaron and I kept silent. After dinner my father drove us to a hotel I had booked in town. We returned to London the next day to stay with a friend of my mother.

Despite witnessing how badly Maureen had treated my father, I felt the trip had been successful. I had bridged a gap with Aaron meeting his only grandfather, and they had enjoyed each others' company. I thought perhaps a door had opened for more meetings.

A week after we arrived home in Seattle, I received an abrupt formal letter from my father saying Maureen had noticed a small silver snuff box of hers was missing after our visit, and would Aaron please return it.

I grilled Aaron till he was close to tears. I cried. He denied knowing anything about the snuff box. As a young teenager, he could easily have pocketed it, perhaps as a 'souvenir' of his trip to see his Grandpa, perhaps as a gift for a friend, or perhaps to spite Maureen for her behavior. Was he telling the truth? After searching his room and his still half-packed suitcase, I found no trace of the snuff box. He continued to deny he had taken it, and still denies it to this day. Who could I believe? My son, my father, my stepmother? I chose to believe my son.

I wrote back to my father saying I believed Aaron had not taken the snuffbox. He had behaved well, enjoyed meeting his grandfather for the first time and had been inspired by his computer skills. Why would he do anything to jeopardize their relationship? I suggested my father look closer to home to find who may have set us up by accusing Aaron of stealing. I reminded him it was Maureen who had previously sabotaged any hope of a relationship between us.

On Christmas Eve, a letter arrived from my father. I expected it to be a Christmas card, Christmas greetings, and perhaps the usual twenty dollar bill. But the words read: "Due to the circumstances, it is best we have no further contact." Stunned and shocked, I immediately threw the letter into the fireplace and watched it burn.

I continued to send him a yearly Christmas card, with no expectation of a response.

I spoke to my father only one more time, ten years later, when I felt a powerful urge to connect with him. He must have already known he had lung cancer. Maureen answered the phone, then my father came on the line and said in the softest, gentlest, most loving voice, "Hello Lindy." I hadn't heard that name since I was a small child, and he was the only person who had ever called me Lindy. I began to cry, then sobbed so hard it was difficult to speak. The conversation was short; we didn't say much. I was too emotional hearing the loving tone to his voice. I never suspected he was nearing the end of his life.

COLD and weary, I leave the dismal cemetery and wait for a bus back to the train station. A man, also waiting at the bus stop, wears a T-shirt with the word: "Nebraska." I ask if he's visited Nebraska. "Yes," he says, "I lived there a short while." He adds, "Such a desolate place."

Desolate echoes my mood, unresolved and sad, tired of travel, with jet lag sucking me down even further. After barely missing a London train, I wait for the next one on a cold metal seat in the drafty waiting room. On the train, dozens of high-pitched teenage voices, chattering, giggling and laughing on their way home from school irritate me. Luckily they get off at the next station. But then, at each slight stop all the way to London, an annoying synthetic voice announces over the intercom: "a signal delay" or "we're on the move again"—as if it isn't obvious—and robotically repeats my location in the train, "this is coach number nine of twelve."

I can hardly wait for the next day, a day off from my quest, with no plans, no schedule and no need to excavate raw emotions of the past. I consider my options. I could take the tube to find the address of the house where I was born; I could visit my grandparent's old home in North London. But no, I decide not to go to either place. I need a day far from the history of my family-of-origin. There are many other choices of places to visit, some with memories, and some I had no interest in visiting while living in England but would now welcome the opportunity to see.

The train pulls into Victoria Station. Again, I struggle against a tide of rush hour crowds, this time office workers leaving the city. I figure out the best way to cut through the crush is to find and follow someone a little taller and wider who parts the crowd. I laugh when I think perhaps there is a life lesson in that. I realize how much happier I feel when I find someone or something larger than the 'little me' when dealing with the outside world, whether a physical being or a belief, and they, or the entire universe, watch out for me and guide my way.

# SATURDAY

I WAKE up late, grateful for a day with no serious cemetery visits, and no soul-searching evaluation of the past.

Benny, the big-hearted owner of Benny's Bed and Breakfast in Ealing fixes breakfast of scrambled eggs and a croissant, sits at my table, then mesmerizes me with stories from his life. What a blessing and a relief to listen to someone else's tales as a change from the jumble of personal stories running through my brain.

He tells me how his mother, after a coup in Iraq, had been told by her husband to quickly burn English papers. She picked up a bundle of old English newspapers lying in a corner and burned them in the backyard. A week later, her distraught husband said he'd found a way to escape from the country if they had their English documents, but now it was too late since he'd told her to destroy their English papers. "No," she replied, smiling, "I misunderstood. I burned English newspapers. It's not too late." They were able to leave the country and move to England.

Benny suggests a visit to Kew Gardens, not far from the Bed and Breakfast. What a perfect suggestion. I never visited the iconic gardens when I lived in London, but as I grow older, I've gained an ever-increasing appreciation of the beauty and healing power of plants and nature.

A silken sky and light drizzle soften the sullen morning. On a quiet Saturday, the big-city weekday decibel level has eased and few people are out early. After hectic plane, tube, bus and train travel, I'm grateful for a vacation day. The lumbering slow double-decker bus to Kew doesn't come anywhere close to hectic.

At Kew, inside the palm house, I stop in awe in front of a giant palm-like tree, now extinct in the wild, a Cycad from

138

South Africa brought to the gardens in 1775, putting in perspective the 'here today, gone tomorrow' world of humans. I imagine how crowds back then were dressed as they wandered through the greenhouse, the first Europeans to admire an exotic tree growing so far from its native land. The palm house is a larger-than-life, living, breathing, sweating plant museum. After half-an-hour I leave the impressive old tropical trees and wander over to an orchid installation in another greenhouse, the Princess of Wales Conservatory.

Approaching lunchtime, with little to do on a gray late-winter Saturday, Londoners have now arrived in droves to view the extraordinary orchid exhibit. So much for escaping crowds. Loud birdsong bursts from somewhere overhead near the glassed-in ceiling—the same birdsong I heard the day before at my father's cemetery! Now I am convinced it must be recorded. Virtual birdsong.

The loud birdsong might be virtual, but cascades of flamboyant orchids tumbling from damp moss beds are intensely real. The displays of lush jungle vegetation, waterfalls, and color are spectacular, breathtaking, and the heady scent hypnotic; but it is all too falsely sweet, too colorful, too moist, and too warm. Within minutes, sensory overload threatens to overwhelm me. Aisles are packed with visitors who 'ooh and aah' and babble incessantly. I breathe deep slow breaths to calm myself as I stroll through the fantasy world, wondering what it must feel like for the plants to be packed together so tightly, stared at, and commented on like animals in a zoo, domesticated and over-fertilized in this claustrophobic orgy of a simulated tropical paradise. I imagine the plants long for spacious freedom, diversity, excitement and danger of a vine-filled rainforest jungle where insects vie for their fair share of fruit and nectar, while overhead a real chorus of exotic birds echoes through the leafy green canopy.

I hurry to an exit. Outside, relieved, I breathe in the freshness of the cool, damp London day.

Simple arrangements of tropical flowers in my mother's house were elegant, aesthetic and spare, never overwhelming. I think back to the introspective quiet cemeteries I visited over the last two days, far more peaceful in a deeply soulful way, and in many ways more satisfying than the hot-house intensity of Kew. Now I look forward to Monday when I travel to the cemetery where I will visit my brother's grave for the first time.

I walk miles through Kew gardens along paths lined with daffodils and crocuses, admiring huge oaks that have shaded the manicured lawns for centuries, enjoying the gentleness of the cool afternoon. When I'm ready to leave, I catch another red double-decker bus back to South Ealing and climb the winding steps to the empty upper deck. Sitting on the front seat at tree level, I feel like I am on top of the world, looking down over the Thames as the bus crosses the famous river.

# SUNDAY

ON Sunday, I visit my only contact who had known my father, Maureen's nephew. Maybe, as much as I needed further understanding, compassion and completion with my father, I need to come to peace with Maureen. Perhaps her nephew has clues.

Two years ago, I had unexpectedly received an email from a stranger in England: "Please could you tell me if you are related to Collings in the UK." Excited, I wondered if a lawyer had sent the email. Perhaps my father or Maureen had softened and left me a small token, a letter or even a small inheritance. But it was ten years since my father had died, and it didn't seem likely.

The email was from Chrissie, the wife of Maureen's nephew, David. When Maureen passed away, ten years after my father, Chrissie and David discovered a box of my father's belongings when they cleared out Maureen's home. Inside the box they found a letter with my name and return address on the envelope. Chrissie, interested in genealogy and mindful of the importance of family history, tracked me down online to see if I might be interested in the contents of the box. She then emailed me a list of the contents. After I chose what I wanted mailed, Chrissie sent the box and invited me to visit them if I ever came to England.

Two years later, in England, I am on my way to lunch with Chrissie and David, hoping more will be revealed about my father. After my dismal visit to Chichester cemetery, any insights to lift my spirits will be most welcome.

Light rain falls from a steely sky. On the nearly empty tube to Paddington Station Sunday morning, the passengers look weary and resigned. Paddington Station is also almost deserted; the quiet station feels hollow and ghostly, resting from the rush

141

and bustle of weekday traffic. Pigeons own the place, strutting aimlessly across the paved marble floor checking for crumbs. Echoing the mournful, depressing tone, I wonder half-heartedly what crumbs I might gather on today's journey.

Luckily, my melancholy mood soon shifts and brightens on the comfortable rapid train ride to Twyford. Butterfly bush and blackberry vines tangle in cascades down slopes of rail-side embankments and golden showers of early Scotch broom bloom extravagantly to light a gray day. At Southall station the sign is in both Hindi and English. A fast, comfortable train, the sight of nature gone wild, a sign in a foreign language—I see all as omens for a good day to visit an English family I have yet to meet.

After greeting me at the station, David drives us through narrow hedge-lined back roads to a delightful country house he and Chrissie built after buying a field in 1971. David says he is in the process of closing down a chauffeured limousine service which, at one time, ran twenty limos; in the course of his long career he drove presidents, Middle Eastern royalty, rock stars, and dignitaries from all over the world, and had gathered hundreds of stories to share. He shares one about President Reagan. While the President waited in David's limo outside a building while a security sweep was in progress, he entertained David for thirty minutes with non-stop dirty jokes.

After Chrissie had graciously mailed the box of my father's belongings, more of his possessions came to light when David cleared out his business garage. Now, while we sit in their elegant living room, David brings out a box full of old pipes my father had never thrown away. Nauseating sweet smells of pipe smoke and bitter stale tobacco come flooding back. As a lifelong pipe smoker, my father suffered from emphysema and died of lung cancer. Had his primary relationship been with his pipe, sucking on the wood, breathing the toxic smoke, while the calming in-breath became an addictive habit? Had the habit been a comforting buffer between him and the world? Especially, between him and Maureen?

David only met my father, Maurice, a few times, since he seldom saw Maureen until after Maurice passed away. Chrissie never met him. Maureen lived for ten years after my father's death and died at the age of ninety-six. David remembers my father as academically brilliant, both inventive and practical, a man who enjoyed both playing creatively on the computer as well as tinkering and fixing everyday gadgets. He brings out a box filled with old tobacco tins my father had painted and fashioned into light-switch plates and Christmas ornaments. I also remembered my father as a skilled craftsman who built tables and cabinets for his house in Spain.

I think back to the only serious conversation I remember with my father. It was during my short fateful visit to him and Maureen in Spain. The conversation was also short.

"What is the greatest virtue?" he asked.

"Truth," I replied. At the time I was an idealistic seeker of Truth, not knowing then the impossibility of a definition.

"No," he said emphatically. "It's Tolerance."

End of conversation. I had been shut down by the "no," implying he was right and I was wrong. I didn't argue the point. Didn't Truth encompass Tolerance? From my radical standpoint back then, tolerance seemed like a wishy-washy virtue that didn't aim high enough, a compromise that didn't contain the whole picture; a cop-out allowing my father to sit back and watch the show. And how did tolerance equate with his statement he could never forgive my mother for marrying him, knowing as he did about her sexual preference? Later, I thought perhaps it was tolerance that enabled him to be married for almost sixty years—twenty-four years to my mother and then thirty-five years to Maureen. I recently listened to a radio interview with a woman who had been married for eighty-four years. When asked how she had managed such a long marriage, she replied, "Tolerance."

Knowing I experienced difficulties with Maureen, David assures me I was not the only one. Maureen had a reputation for being territorial, particularly around her kitchen, and was known for her imperious nature and impatience. I am happy to hear I wasn't the only one to witness the vindictive side of Maureen's personality. How else could my father have lived with that, except through tolerance?

David brings out another box, containing music-mix cassette tapes and ten large sheets of paper covered with small neat handwriting. My father had painstakingly catalogued, down to the exact minute and seconds on the tapes, playlists of an extensive library of songs and music he and Maureen had enjoyed. He had lovingly compiled and recorded their favorite music for Maureen to listen to after his death.

Chrissie serves an appetizing spaghetti meal with a green salad, and for dessert, homemade blackberry and apple pie, made with berries and apples from their garden. I am grateful for the healthy home-cooked meal after days of eating greasy fast food from delis and Indian snack shops that have replaced newspaper and tobacconist stands next to London tube stations.

Then David shares by far the most poignant and unique information. Over the years, Maurice and Maureen recorded their conversations—nothing special, everyday casual conversations, as a gift for whoever outlived the other. What an amazing way for a surviving spouse to relive memories of their loved one and their lives together through the sound of everyday conversations! When David visited Maureen during the ten years after Maurice's death, she often came out of a room smiling, saying she'd been spending time with Maurice, meaning she'd been listening to their taped conversations.

David thought he had saved the tapes in a box somewhere, but in the chaos of his move had misplaced them; he promised to mail them to me if they turned up. But they were never found. What a touching goldmine of information that would have been!

David tells an anecdote of how he had taken Maureen for a visit to a hospital, and overheard a nurse ask her what she would like to be called. When Maureen seemed confused, the nurse asked, "What did your husband call you?"

"Darling," she replied.

So there it was. What I had been looking for. Something positive. A love story.

I had begun the day hoping for something to transform my understanding of my father. Although I never had a chance to reconcile with him when he was alive, how could I not be happy and grateful that, even if I had briefly witnessed otherwise, perhaps Maurice and Maureen had been a devoted couple who found love, healing, and companionship with each other for the second half of their lives?

# MONDAY

ON Monday I visit my brother Christopher's grave for the first time. Fifty years after his death.

I wake before dawn, stow everything in my small pack, and leave the Ealing Bed and Breakfast. The weather has turned frosty with an icy wind, and I again wonder if it foretells how events of the day will unfold, although yesterday's gloomy weather didn't affect the warmth and hospitality received from David and Chrissie.

Why investigate affairs of the dead? Why dig up feelings that silenced questions I never asked either parent for fear of causing further grief and suffering? Why now?

I have finally reached an age when I have the time, curiosity, courage and detachment to dive deeper into the details of a pivotal event in my life.

Nine years of boarding school had silenced and deadened me, and then Christopher's suicide shocked me back to life, to emotional highs and lows, plus awakened, through grief, conscious awareness of the interiority of my own being, prompting me to seek an independent path in life, which did not include my family of origin.

So many years later, with a clear mind and open heart, I am ready to re-visit a time I knew little about, or sought to understand, when younger.

Commuters crowd the rush hour tube to Paddington train station. The station buzzes with the vibrant hum of a busy Monday morning commute. Hollow ghosts of the previous day have slunk back into the shadows; pigeons no longer roam the platforms but perch high overhead keeping watch over the bustling scene. All seats on the train to Hereford are taken; then, at Oxford Station, the train empties. I settle in for the three hour ride through early spring countryside, watching field after field of young lambs frolicking, bouncing, stumbling on wobbly legs, or nestled close to their freshly shorn mothers. Honeybourne, Moreton-on-Marsh, then the rolling green Malvern Hills.

Back in January I began an online search for either my brother's burial place, or his ashes. My only clue was a death certificate my stepmother, Maureen, had sent along with a few photographs and papers after my father passed away. Christopher's death certificate said nothing about his burial place, only where his body was found, in the Welsh village of Llangattock, next to the town of Crickhowell, with the cause of death: "Cyanide poisoning. Self-administered while the balance of his mind was disturbed." An inquest had been held on May 24$^{th}$ 1962, presided over by the Coroner for the County of Brecon.

I found a website for the District Archive Center in the town of Crickhowell. A series of emails to the Center also found a record of the same death certificate, but failed to find documentation of the inquest, and again drew a blank with the location of a grave site. Then a volunteer at the Archive Center sent this advice: "There's no record of a cremation at the local crematorium, or burial in local graveyards. Note: he would have been interned in unconsecrated ground due to the suicide. This indicates he was removed from the area to the most likely family home place." Had his body been taken to the Brighton cemetery closer to my mother's home, where her ashes were later scattered? I emailed Brighton crematorium but they had no record of my brother.

The Archive Center then referred me to Powys County Archives Office in Llandrindod Wells. They too were unable to fulfill my request for a copy of the inquest report, but recommended I contact a Library where there might be files of old Breckonshire newspapers, in particular the 'Brecon-Times

Gazette', a newspaper in existence for only two years, from 1961 to 1963. The Powys office also suggested Christopher might have been cremated or buried in England, outside the Welsh border, in the town of Hereford.

I was almost ready to give up, but the Library staff were hopeful, and helpful. After searching through the old newspapers they found a story on the inquest which they forwarded to me. Progress. But there was no mention of a burial place in that article either, although the report listed many other details, including names of people close to Christopher around the time of his death. A Google search turned up information on the name of one man, mentioned in the inquest, who had been my brother's roommate when he died, and now owned a company in Hereford. Maybe he would know where my brother was buried. Other names in the report were too common to find through Google. I contacted the man in Hereford by emailing his company and received a note back from the man's son saying his father had died, but he remembered his father mentioning, more than once, how he had attempted, unsuccessfully, to resuscitate a fellow student, my brother. The man's son did not know where my brother was buried.

I perhaps had a clue though, from the Powys office. The town of Hereford. My mother sometimes traveled to Hereford to stay with a distant cousin. Of course! Maybe my mother not only visited her cousin, but also the grave of her son. A request for records from the Hereford Cemetery confirmed that, yes, my brother was, indeed, buried there; he had not been cremated, but his bones were interred in a grave at the cemetery.

☼

IN the taxi from Hereford station to the Cemetery, as we drive past the Bulmers cider factory, the paunchy red-faced driver jokes, with a gentle lilting West Country accent, "We call cider Tanglefoot. Drink too much and you'll fall over your feet." Perhaps he knows from experience, or has given rides to many a late night customer with tangled feet.

I leave my travel bag at the desk of the Cemetery office and pick up a map marked with the location of my brother's grave. Except for distant sounds of a backhoe digging a grave in a far corner, the cemetery is deserted. The sound stops. What a relief. I am also relieved there's no recorded birdsong in this quiet cemetery. Already, a fierce, cold wind blows through the cemetery and I don't need further aggravation to disturb my increasingly nervous state.

I wander up and down poorly marked aisles until I arrive at a stone cross on top of a tilted headstone. The inscription reads: "In Memory of Christopher Hope Collings. Born 30th May 1943. Died 1st April 1962." So simple. I am surprised to see the cross, the only one in the row of headstones. I guess the cross must have been my mother's choice, not the choice of my atheist father. I wonder though, why no one thought to put the words 'In Loving Memory of,' instead of 'In Memory of.' Perhaps my parents believed his death had been an act of violence directed at them, and the wound too deep, the guilt and shame still festering as the sculptor applied his chisel to the stone, and it was too late to change the wording. Or maybe, as echoed in the engraved words, Christopher never received the love he needed and deserved either in his lifetime or beyond.

Shaking slightly, I drop to the cold ground and kneel at the foot of the grave. This is the first time I have visited a grave containing a relative's bones. The scattered ashes of my parents hadn't had the same effect.

Wiping warm tears from my cheeks, I open the space for an internal imagined conversation with my long-dead brother. Unexpectedly, he begins the conversation.

"What took you so long to visit, little sis? My bones have been lying here a long, long while." His voice is surprisingly light and playful.

"But, I'm here now, big brother. I didn't know where you were buried. And I didn't ask. I should have."

"I know, little sis. Mom should have told you. I'm so sorry for the pain I caused."

"It's okay; it was a long time ago and it woke me up."

I had always looked to my big brother for approval. "Christopher, are you proud of me for what I've done in my life?"

"Of course I'm proud of you, little sis."

I let the words sink in as tears flow freely down my face.

From my pocket I pull out a handful of rose petals I have brought with me from my home altar, and stuff the petals carefully into cracks where the headstone meets the ground. I don't want them blowing away in the cold wind, at least, not right away.

My brother continues the conversation. "I screwed up. It was all I knew to do. It was a different time. And maybe what I cracked open wasn't all bad—look at Dad's love affair and long marriage to Maureen. And Mom had some good times and freedom, plus you gave her a grandson she adored. Your life blossomed. You broke away to look for the answers you needed for your own life."

Tears turn cold as they streak my wind-chilled cheeks. "I'm sorry for whatever terrible pain you must have suffered that made you decide to take your life with no one to turn to. Tomorrow, maybe I'll find out more about what happened and why you did it."

"Yes, maybe you will. Thank you, little sis, for making this journey."

Tiny darts of dry snow driven by an icy wind begin to spit diagonal against my face. Inwardly I chant a healing mantra for the dead as I sit quietly by the grave. I lose all sense of time. But, slowly, the freezing wind drills right through my clothes and into my bones, forcing me to get up from the cold ground and leave the grave site before I freeze.

Back at the cemetery office to pick up my bag, the man at the desk asks, "Got it all sorted have you?"

"Yep, but if I stayed any longer, shivering in the bitter wind, I'd soon be underground too."

"It's been a quiet week," he says, "we could fit you in…"

We both laugh. A sense of humor must be an essential requirement for cemetery workers.

I TAKE a taxi back to the station, then a train to Abergavenny where I wait in the station café for another taxi to Llangattock, the small village where my brother died. The man behind the counter strikes up a conversation, and when he finds out I'm visiting from America, tells me how he's been to Oklahoma, Mississippi, New Mexico, New York and last year, Aspen. Not bad for someone who runs a small railway station café in Wales. I tell him my brother had trained as an apprentice chemist at the steelworks near Abergavenny at Ebbw Vale after winning a scholarship to study Physics at Cambridge University. "Ah yes," he says with a soft Welsh accent, "that steelworks, it's all been flattened now."

The taxi driver greets me with "Aw right darlin' where ya goin' now?" The easy friendliness of people in this part of the world rings straight to my heart. In Llangattock, the taxi drops me off at The Olde Six Bells Bed and Breakfast. The Inn, three joined stone cottages built in 1680, was a pub for a hundred years before its current incarnation as a Bed and Breakfast.

I planned to visit several pubs in the small village, hoping to talk to old timers who might remember the scandalous suicide from many years ago, and, if luck was with me, find and meet the woman mentioned in my brother's inquest report.

At dusk I wander down the ancient narrow street from the Olde Six Bells to The Horseshoe Inn, now the only pub still in existence in the old village. At one time, every corner housed a pub, but with the closure of coal mines and steel mills, miners and steel workers moved away, and the population plummeted. From the inquest report I knew Christopher had visited The Horseshoe Inn on the evening of his death.

In the window, a small sign reads: 'Closed on Monday nights'.

The moon is almost full, the wind quiet. At sunset, by the Usk River I wander under ragged pink clouds through fields bordered by rough-hewn stone walls, feeling at peace, ready for whatever unsolved mysteries or surprises the next day will bring. Perhaps I will discover nothing and simply spend time meandering through the picturesque small Welsh village where my brother chose to end his life.

Back at the Bed and Breakfast, after a long hot shower and the pleasure of the most luxurious thick-piled snow-white bath towel I have ever known, I sink into the softest feather bed I have ever slept in, feeling well-nourished by the comforting environment, my heart soft and vulnerable from the visit to my brother's grave.

# TUESDAY

SUNLIGHT streams through gauze curtains as I wake from a sleep so deep and dreamless, I feel reborn. A light frost glitters on slate-tiled rooftops.

I have only one day to investigate circumstances surrounding my brother's death.

After a hearty breakfast fixed by Richard, the owner of the Olde Six Bells, I cross the ancient River Usk Bridge and hike up the steep, winding lanes leading to the town of Crickhowell where I stop in at the District Archive Center, hoping to find the two men I had corresponded with online. I want to thank them for their help and to make a donation, but neither man is a volunteer today. Instead, I talk briefly with a woman who tells me the village of Llangattock was known in the nineteenth century for the longevity of its inhabitants, when it was common for people to live into their nineties, even their hundreds. Many elderly inhabitants attributed their long lives to drinking rejuvenating spring water from the surrounding hills, while others attributed longevity to the abundance of local pubs. Maybe my brother would have lived longer if he had chosen to drink the rejuvenating spring water. Perhaps he would still be alive.

Knowing I can learn nothing more from the District Archives, I hike back down to Llangattock and visit the old stone church of St Catwgs beside the Bed and Breakfast. Part of the building's foundation dates back to the 6th century, while the oldest section of the present building dates back to the 12th century. Sitting in an old wooden pew at the back of the church, I sink into the pressing weight of silence rich with hundreds of years of history and muttered prayer. I wonder if Christopher ever visited this church. Probably not. I don't remember seeing him show an interest in religion.

At noon, I wander down to The Horseshoe Inn hoping to meet the perfect person for my quest enjoying a lunchtime pint. But when I step through the old doorway into the dark low-ceilinged pub and look around, I see I am the only customer. I chat briefly with a young Asian girl behind the bar, Ivy, who tells me she and her husband bought the business only a year ago. How stupid of me to think the same owners might still be there fifty years later. I order a bowl of hearty potato leek soup, sit at a table, and wait, watching for someone old to walk through the door, my expectations dropping by the minute. I had imagined Welsh pubs to be thriving local hangouts, especially for an aging population. I am beginning to think my plans might have come to a dead end. At 12:30pm I am still the only person in the room. Ivy brings my soup.

"Do any old timers visit the pub at this time of day?"

"Yes, on Tuesdays three elderly gentlemen meet here for lunch. One in his nineties, two in their eighties."

"Today's Tuesday. Do they always come?"

"Almost always. I don't know why they're not here today."

So close. I decide to wait a while longer and see if anyone shows up. At 1:00pm, I am still the only customer.

At 1:10pm the pub door swings open and in walks an elderly man. He heads directly to the bar and orders a whiskey. I guess he must be in his eighties, which would put him around thirty-years-old fifty years ago. With luck, the tall, elegantly dressed, slightly elfin-looking man has lived in the village all his life, and with an excellent memory, remembers everyone and everything that has happened here. Wishful thinking. The Asian girl catches my eye, and with a slight nod lets me know the man is one of the regular old timers.

I am not shy. I walk up to the bar and introduce myself to the sprightly man.

He shakes my hand. "Alwyn. Means 'wise and magical friend,' or 'friend of the elves,'" he says with the sweetest smile. "I'll be ninety-five next week."

Yes! Here is my connection. With a name like that, no wonder he looks elfin despite his height. Ninety-five! With his youthful looks and longevity, he must have been drinking the spring water, although with the speed he downed his whiskey, it's more likely the pubs. "Did you live in Llangattock in 1962?"

"Sorry, not back then. We moved to the village in 1984."

Another dead end. Whenever I think I might be getting closer, I am wrong.

"But my neighbors are from here." He adds with a cheerful grin, "I can take you up there and introduce you if you like. After I wait for my friends."

My level of hope bounces up and down like a yoyo. "That would be great. Thank you."

He offers me a whiskey. I decline, wanting to keep a clear head for what could be an intense few hours ahead. He throws back another shot. I sit beside him at the bar and tell him briefly about my brother's death and my desire to know more. Then, while he waits for his friends, he holds me spellbound with stories from his own long life.

Some of his friends call him 'Lived Twice'.

Gifted with second sight, he'd had a vision of his death near the end of World War Two, to the exact date and time. A year later, on the predicted day, he was declared dead in wartime action during an Italian winter. He had reached up to grab one of his soldiers out of the line of fire, only to be zapped by flying shrapnel. Bleeding profusely, he was pronounced dead and his body thrown into the back of an open truck in freezing weather. Blood froze over the wounds and stopped the bleeding during the five hundred kilometer drive to a military hospital.

The freezing weather saved his life. When they reached the hospital, he awoke. During his 'death' journey he had experienced visions of himself in a previous lifetime at Epidavros, the ancient Greek center for medicine in the fifth century BC, where he was given the gift of miraculous healing.

He downs a third whiskey. "Looks like my friends aren't going to make it today. I'll drive you up to visit my neighbors. Plus show you where your brother lived and died, right around the corner from my house. I moved here because of that place. After the hostel closed, for years it was a nursing home and treatment center for people with ALS, Lou Gehrig's disease. We moved here for my wife. She's completely disabled with ALS. The place closed a month ago. Now I'm her caretaker."

At ninety-five, a caretaker for his disabled wife! And still driving!

How strange the feng shui of the building where Christopher died must be. His death certificate says he'd died 'while the balance of his mind was disturbed.' I wonder whether the minds of people suffering from ALS are disturbed.

Getting into a stranger's car in a foreign country isn't something I would normally do, especially since this particular stranger has tossed back several whiskeys and is ninety-five years old. But today is not normal. I am seeking answers to questions of life and death in a few short hours, and this spry old man with a magical name has appeared as a perfect ally to assist in my search. I ease into Alwyn's tiny car, making sure my seat belt is securely fastened, while he, without fastening his seat belt, drives slowly up the hill to his neighbors' house. I ask him if he is concerned about either drunk driving or not wearing a seat belt. He isn't. He tells me police are rarely seen in Llangattock, except in summer when visitors overrun the tiny picturesque village.

156

Alwyn's neighbors, a kind elderly couple, invite us in and offer tea and cookies to the foreigner visiting from America.

"Yes," the man says, "we were both born in this village, but left for several years and didn't come back here till the mid 1960s. That would have been after your brother's death."

"Maybe you know someone who lived here then?" I ask.

"You should go visit Alwyn's friend, Peter. He's lived here forever."

"Of course! He's one of my friends who didn't show up at the pub today. I'll take you to see him. He lives two doors away from Onney House, the house you mentioned in your brother's inquest report."

Christopher had visited Onney House the night of his death. Earlier today, I had noticed Onney House, empty, with a 'For Sale' sign out front. The inquest report listed the house as the home of Mrs. Barbara Tomlinson, who offered an 'open invitation' to visit her home to the twelve apprentices at Llangattock Park House Hostel before they left to study at Cambridge. The night Christopher died, he and other students visited her house after an evening at the Horseshoe Inn. I am almost certain Barbara must be the woman in some way involved in his death.

The inquest report also mentioned a writing pad had been found on Christopher's bed next to his body. The coroner, holding up the pad for the inquest jury to see, stated he would not read aloud what was written on the pad, adding, "To my mind, it is purely personal and nothing is to be gained by reading it out." Who were the words for? Were they written to Barbara? Was my brother in love with her? What did his final words say? I want to find and speak to Barbara. I keep my fingers crossed she is alive and still lives in the area.

We squeeze back into Alwyn's tiny car. Before heading to his friend Peter's house, we drive to the building where

Christopher ended his life, previously Llangattock Park House Hostel, now privately owned by a wealthy business man. Alwyn had had an earlier falling out with the owner, and as soon as we drive into the parking lot, a surly man strides up to the car and barks words at Alwyn when he rolls down his window. Previously, I thought I might want to go inside the house, but now have no desire to enter; the vibe of the building and owner are too weird. Alwyn is shaken and flustered by the encounter. We leave quickly without getting out of the car. His driving deteriorates. The tiny vehicle bucks and jerks as he changes gears and hurries to back down the driveway. "You're getting me all hot and bothered," he says with a big grin.

We head back downhill to his friend Peter's cottage. Peter is home. When he opens the front door, a noxious blast of oil paint and turpentine hits us, the odor so thick it's almost visible. I step back, take a deep breath, then enter the small cottage. Peter's oil paintings cover every inch of wall and corner of the living room. In the center of the room an easel holds a half-finished landscape. I am amazed how the man has survived to be eighty-five years old in an environment where the smell of paint has seeped into every piece of furniture and crack in the wall. Once again it must be the Llangattock spring water, the elixir of old age, keeping him alive.

"Sorry I never made it at lunchtime to the Inn," Peter says to Alwyn, "this picture wouldn't let me go. What are you up to, you old goat, visiting me with this lovely young lady?"

I retell my brother's story.

Peter recalls how apprentices came to the village on college scholarships to work at the steel works for a year and remembers the tragic suicide of one of the boys. He had known Barbara Tomlinson's family with their four or five children.

Yes! My first lucky break.

"Barbara was very attractive, a real looker. Her husband was an architect." He looks pensive, slowly searching through memories of a time long gone. "There were rumors she was more than a friend to some of the students. Maybe your brother? I think she was pregnant at the time. The family moved away from Onney House soon after."

My brain does a flip. Pregnant? What are the chances I have a niece or nephew? Was that why my brother killed himself? "Do you know where they went?"

"I don't know where they went. I'll check the phone book."

There are no Tomlinsons listed in the phone book.

"You know who might know: John Edwards. He knows everyone and everything ever happened around here. Been here forever. Lives down the road between Onney House and The Horseshoe Inn."

Onward with the quest.

Alwyn drops me in front of an old stone terraced house next to the pub. He has to leave to take care of his wife. Very grateful for his help, we say a warm goodbye. Even if today turns out to be a wild goose chase, I have been blessed to meet such kind-hearted people, especially the elfin Alwyn.

A middle-aged woman, John's daughter, answers the door to John's house and invites me in. Once again, I tell my story. Between John and his daughter, I learn Barbara died six or seven years ago. They think they remember Barbara giving birth to another child, her fifth, after Christopher's death.

"I knew Jane Tomlinson, one of Barbara's older children," says John's daughter. "She had a clothing shop in Crickhowell for a long time, but the shop closed several months ago. Jane's still in the area but I don't know where."

Again, so close.

"But wait, I have a friend, Lucy, who worked for Jane for years. She'd know how to contact her. Lucy works at the opticians in Crickhowell now—she's probably still there. The shop closes at five today."

I check my watch. At twenty minutes before five, is it possible to reach the store before closing? I have to decide fast whether to drop my quest then, or, through Lucy, see if I can make contact with Barbara's daughter, Jane. If I am an aunt, I want to know! It is a situation of 'now or never'.

"Thank you so much!" I rush out the door.

I jog back across the old stone Usk Bridge, huff and pant up the narrow lanes of the hill into Crickhowell and find the optician shop near the center of town. I push open the door at 4:55pm.

Lucy stands behind the counter, getting ready to close the store.

Out of breath, I hurriedly explain my mission of looking for Jane Tomlinson, and that I leave the area in the morning to head back to the United States. I hand Lucy the inquest report. She makes a copy and says she knows how to contact Jane, but doesn't feel free to give out Jane's phone number; she takes my number at the Olde Six Bells.

"I'll pass along the information. If Jane remembers anything and feels okay with what you told me, I'll tell her to call you this evening."

"If she doesn't want to call me, here's my email address, in case she decides to contact me later. Thank you so much."

I retreat down the hill and back over the Usk Bridge, then take a shortcut on a footpath across a field. Near the path, a farmer has built a small bonfire to burn an uprooted tree stump. The fire has almost died; wisps of smoke curl slowly from the charred wood, while last glowing embers smolder close to the ground. Nearing the end of my visit to the UK, I think of Indian funeral pyres, letting go of the dead, and how perhaps this stump fire symbolizes the burning of residual karmas still clinging to my family of origin.

☼

BACK at the Bed and Breakfast, exhausted, and at the same time, excited, I flop down on my bed. I had never imagined the unlikely possibility of finding a relative on this short trip. What if my brother had fathered a child with Barbara? Would the birth have lessened the tragedy of his death, whatever his reasons for taking his life? I also wonder, if a child of his had been born, wouldn't my mother have been notified that she was a grandmother? I wait, and hope, for a phone call from Jane, but know, too, perhaps Jane might not want to revisit that time, if she even remembers it.

At seven o'clock Richard knocks on my door. "There's a phone call for you downstairs. A woman called Jane."

Yes! Progress! I race down the narrow spiral stone staircase.

"Hello Jane, this is Nirvan. Thank you so much for calling. I'm so glad you responded to my message." My heart beats fast. "I wondered if you remember anything about the death of my brother, if there's anything you can tell me."

"Yes, I remember that time well, though I was young. It was a terrible tragedy. I'll tell you what I know."

"Thank you again. And I'm sorry to hear of the death of your mother."

"Thank you. About that time. We were an artistic, bohemian family, outsiders. We moved to the village a couple of years before your brother's death. My mother had been to art school and considered herself an artist. She befriended the scholarship apprentices, boys who were also outsiders in the village—most of whom were from well-off, well-educated families, not like most of the locals. She called them the Park Boys, and they knew her as Bobbie, or Babs. They were always welcomed into the warmth of our home. Our house was full of life; my brothers and sisters loved and adored the Park Boys."

I can barely wait to ask my important question. "Someone told me today your mother gave birth to a fifth child around that time. Is it possible I have a relative?"

"No, you're not an aunt." Jane pauses. "My mother never had an affair with any of the boys. It was my father who had affairs. It was my father's child."

"Oh," I sigh, deflated. My imagination had run away with me. Why then did Barbara play a role in the inquest?

"Did you not know your brother was gay?"

I am stunned. How could that be? Not only did I not have another relative, but I hadn't known my brother was gay. Yet another example of how blind I had been. "No, I didn't know."

"He came out during the week before he died."

"Was he in love with one of the other students? Was that why he killed himself?"

"No, I don't think so."

"Did you know Christopher?"

"Yes, I knew him, we called him Chris. He was sweet and quiet."

"What did your mother have to do with his death? Why was she questioned at the inquest?"

"My mother was a confidante, a close friend to many of the boys, as she was to Chris. Your brother was often depressed, but never mentioned anything about ending his life." She pauses. "Early on the evening of his death, Chris phoned my mother, saying he wanted to talk to her about something important. She replied she didn't have time. She regretted that her whole life. My mother was devastated by what happened."

"I'm so sorry. How awful. She must have been busy with her children."

"Yes, I'm sure she was just busy at that particular moment, because she always tried to make time for the boys. After the phone call, Chris went out drinking with his friends at the Inn, and then he and several others stopped by our house. Nobody noticed anything unusual about him; he was his usual quiet self. I do remember though that sometime during the evening one of the boys made a stupid comment specifically aimed at Chris—I won't mention names."

Jane then tells me almost all the Park Boys from that group are now dead, except for one who became a well known global arms dealer. I suspect it was he who made the cruel comment—a man who later became an international bully.

I want to know about the note on the writing pad.

"The inquest report states Christopher left your house alone, just before midnight, saying he had letters to write. The coroner showed a pad, found on Christopher's bed, to the jury, and said: 'To my mind, the note is purely personal and nothing is to be gained by reading it out.' Do you know if the note was addressed to your mother?"

"I don't remember my mother mentioning a note. But then, she was so desperately upset, and probably wouldn't have told us. We were all upset. I think if she had kept the note, it would be with her papers that went to her second husband after she died. I'll ask him."

"Thank you so much Jane, you've been a great help. I had no idea my brother was gay."

"If anything turns up in the future I can let you know."

I LIE on my soft feather bed, digesting the news. For several hours I had been thrilled by the possibility of my brother fathering a child, another relative to add to my small family.

Now, I feel unexpectedly disappointed, deeply sad, and empty. The heartbreaking news that he took his life because he was gay, alone, and depressed, adds a new tragic dimension to my family history.

My mother had told me that a week before killing himself, Christopher wrote to Cambridge University telling them he no longer wanted to accept his scholarship. All my father's hopes had been placed on Christopher following in his footsteps to Cambridge University.

How terribly my father must have suffered at the time, and how he must have blamed my mother for being gay and perhaps causing Christopher's death, thinking she must have passed the 'gay gene' down to her son, as some believed at that time. It is much easier now for me to understand why, after Christopher died, my father quickly divorced my mother and chose a new life for himself that did not include his former family. How utterly brokenhearted and responsible my mother must have felt for such a family tragedy.

How had I not known my brother was gay? The same way I had not realized my mother was gay; I was blind to the world outside of my small life. My brother had had a girlfriend during school summer vacations, so how could he have been gay? I did remember how he slowly withdrew over the years, spending hours shut in his bedroom listening to classical music, but the word 'depression' wasn't in my vocabulary then. I also remembered how he teased me on a day when he was preparing to return to boarding school, and in retaliation for the teasing, I stood on a second floor landing and tossed perfume onto his hair as he went downstairs—saying I hoped his friends would call him a sissy. How little I knew.

Lying on my bed at the Bed and Breakfast, I realize I haven't eaten for hours. I head back down the narrow street to The Horseshoe Inn for another bowl of potato leek soup. The place is full now, exactly as I'd imagined a low-ceiling Welsh village pub should be. I choose a small table in the corner, wanting to be as inconspicuous as possible, but all eyes turn to stare at me: the visiting American. By now the whole village knows my story. I am reminded of a Welsh saying Alwyn shared earlier in the day: "You know you belong here if they're talking about you." My brother belonged in this village long after his death. I guess I do too now.

# WEDNESDAY

I SAY goodbye to The Olde Six Bells and Llangattock, full of emotion for learning more about my brother, sad to leave the picturesque small village, and also grateful for everything I have experienced during the rollercoaster of the last two days. I take a taxi back to Abergavenny and catch a train to Hereford, only to have to return to Newport in Wales to take the train to London. While waiting on a platform I overhear a conductor answering an inquiry about a schedule delay. He tells a man annoyed by the wait: "A suicide on the tracks. It happens quite often to be honest."

I don't understand suicide. Nothing even comes close to what needs saying, and perhaps that's it—there is no ultimate conclusion, however much I'd wish there to be. It is too wide and broad of a subject. There are too many factors involved, too many variables in each situation, whether well-planned or spontaneous. Circumstances are unique for everyone involved: for those who choose to end their lives; their close family and friends; witnesses, and anyone indirectly affected. But it almost always comes as a tragic shock to those left behind.

In the case of Christopher, had he been born thirty, twenty or even ten years later, would his homosexuality have been less of an issue than in the early 1960s when criminal charges and aversion therapy for sexual preference were not uncommon? I do wonder why he chose such a painful method to die—perhaps it was the ease of access to cyanide he took from the lab where he worked, plus the common knowledge of how swift and fatal the poison would be. Not so many years before, cyanide pills had been the wartime death of choice to avoid capture by the enemy.

And now, in at least two countries in Europe, Belgium and the Netherlands, assisted suicide is available not only to those

166

physically close to death, but also, after a series of rigorous interviews, to those who see no hope or possibility of a livable future for themselves. Perhaps this option could also be acceptable for those who choose to leave, knowing with certainty they have completed their life's work. When a person's desire to leave this life is not treated as an unthinkable religious or criminal act, how much more humane it would be, and how much kinder for all loved ones and friends involved, to face, and come to terms with the person's wishes. There would be an opportunity to support the person with love and compassion for their choice, rather than suffer the shock, guilt, shame, confusion, grieving and sometimes anger experienced by those left behind with no understanding or completion. With the population of the world increasing exponentially and people living longer and longer, perhaps it will not be such a 'taboo' choice in the future. A person could leave the world supported, with dignity and respect.

Questions remain. Did my brother know his mother was gay? Why was he not able to confide in her, or even me? Did either my father or mother know that Christopher was gay? How little I had known him. Years away from home at boarding schools had left the two of us distant, although I always felt his protective influence around me—he was, after all, my big brother, smart and experienced, and I had trusted he would grow up to lead the way to a successful life in the world.

Several years after Christopher's death, I married a man who had attempted suicide. Many years later, long after a divorce, he thanked me for helping him survive, and later thrive, in the world. If I had known what I know now, when Christopher was still alive, perhaps I could have done the same for him.

☼

# THURSDAY

ARRIVING back in London on Wednesday evening, it feels like weeks since I left the Bed and Breakfast in South Ealing, only two days ago.

I sleep soundly. And in the hours before dawn, I dream of wandering at an outdoor music and crafts festival with Christopher by my side. We admire fine jewelry at a crafts booth and sample homemade artisanal cheese at a food booth. A stunningly beautiful, yet unassuming, woman steps onto a stage and sings an aria in a mellow, wide-ranging, rich, and deeply resonant voice. I turn my brother's attention to listen to the singer.

I wake and wonder if there is any significance or meaning to the dream. It feels like a healing dream. Healing for my brother? Can the wounded, depressive, suicidal masculine side be healed by the strong-voiced, versatile, beautiful feminine side within him? Can the living heal the wounds of the dead? I like to believe so, even if only through dreams.

ON the flight to Seattle I look back over the short, full visit to my country of birth. Throughout my journey I felt tremendous gratitude for so many moments of kindness, humor, hospitality, insight and friendship shared by all the generous, helpful and remarkable people I met on my trip to England and Wales.

In the whirlwind ten days from when I walked out of my front door in Tacoma, until arriving home in the Pacific Northwest, I flew on two planes, took four taxi rides, caught six buses, rode in seven cars, took nineteen tube rides, rode on thirteen trains, and walked several miles. I visited disembodied, interred and scattered relatives and dug deep into stories of grief and abandonment, tragedy, sexual identity, and love.

The trip allowed me to gain understanding of why I had been unable to question or absorb much of what had happened around me in my early years, why I chose a life far from the land of my birth, and why many years went by before I chose to dive into the past, to re-visit and learn from the rich, complex and tragic legacy of my family of origin that formed, and still informs, my life today.

# Acknowledgements

FIRST, much gratitude is due to my family of origin, my grandparents, parents and brother. Then to other people mentioned in the book, whether named or not: Tom Coroneos, who knows my story well; three Dons, (Don Walsh, Don Littleton, Don Franklin), Paula, Ali, Fred, Roy, and Alwyn.

Thank you to Yossarian Kelley for his excellent poem at the beginning.

I am very grateful for writing group friends who have enriched my life tremendously with our almost weekly sharings: Randy Kasten, Belinda Moses, Allie Durrie, Nettie Harper, Dianna Timm Dryden, Tree Smith, Carl Anderson, Mark Woytowich, Corrinne McGrady, Elisa Peterson, Kirsten Schowalter, David Snyder and Terry Oliver. And special thanks to Leslie Hatch for her diligent proofing and suggestions. Any errors and flaws still within the book are entirely mine after I made last minute tweaks and changes.

Thank you to dear friends who have read or listened to my stories over the years. Madir Thackeray (especially for the laughter), Carly List, Grace Welker, Hilary Leighton, Dhyanam and Shanti Shivani. I am also grateful for vendor neighbors and market friends entertained by, and curious about, my life and stories: Laurie Mortenson, Michel Tegelenbosch, Tami Sioux, Emily, Engayla, Nora, Leah, Pam, Cat and Lexi.

Gratitude goes to Nikki Smith who originally listened to my proposed 'Trip Back' to England and encouraged my journey, to Gary and Melinda Seelig who kindly gave funding, and to Chrissie Lowe for suggesting there was a story to be told. And love and thanks to my generous son, Aaron, for the gift of airline miles to anywhere in the world that led to a trip to Australia.

And a thank you to Beverly Belville for providing a quiet space to write in her lakeside home. While tapping away at the keyboard I listen to music, mostly ambient: Al Gromer Khan and Klaus Weise, Jonsi and Alex, Steve Roach, Byron Metcalf, Mark Seelig and numerous other artists through Pandora and Bandcamp, thank you.

I am grateful for all my teachers in their various shapes, forms and voices over the years. And finally, much gratitude is due Frank LaRue Owen for the inspiration of his poetry and his role as a muse for the completion of this project.

# About the Author

NIRVAN HOPE is the author of *Three Seasons of Bees and Other Natural and Unnatural Things: a Pacific Northwest Journal, Gypsy Soup: a Novel* and a book of poetry, *Love and the Infinite.* She currently writes from a room overlooking a lake in the South Sound region of Washington State, where she is easily distracted by birds, squirrels, and the occasional coyote who strolls by her window. She is also a photographer.

www.nirvanhope.com

Made in the USA
Columbia, SC
22 April 2019